CU00323042

DOMINIC COOKE

Dominic Cooke adapted and directed the original production of *Arabian Nights* for the Young Vic in 1998, which was followed by both national and international tours and was revived by the RSC in 2009. He also adapted and directed Malorie Blackman's *Noughts & Crosses* for the RSC in 2007, which was followed by a national tour in 2008. His directing work for the Royal Court includes *Aunt Dan and Lemon*, *Wig Out!*, *Now or Later*, *Rhinoceros*, *The Pain and the Itch*, *Other People*, *Fireface*, *Spinning into Butter*, *Redundant*, *Fucking Games*, *Plasticine*, *The People are Friendly*, *This is a Chair*, and *Identical Twins*. Other directing work in the theatre includes *Pericles*, *The Winter's Tale*, *The Crucible*, *Postcards from America*, *As You Like It*, *Macbeth*, *Cymbeline*, *The Malcontent* (RSC); *By the Bog of Cats* (Wyndham's); *The Eccentricities of a Nightingale* (Gate, Dublin); *The Weavers*, *Hunting Scenes From Lower Bavaria* (Gate); *The Bullet* (Donmar); *Afore Night Come*, *Entertaining Mr Sloane* (Clwyd); *The Importance of Being Earnest* (Atlantic Theatre Festival, Canada); *Caravan* (National Theatre of Norway); *My Mother Said I Never Should* (Oxford Stage Co/Young Vic); *Kiss of the Spider Woman* (Bolton Octagon); *Of Mice and Men* (Nottingham Playhouse); and *Autogeddon* (Assembly Rooms). Awards include Laurence Olivier Awards for Best Director and Best Revival 2006 for *The Crucible*; TMA Award 2000 for *Arabian Nights*; Fringe First Award 1991 for *Autogeddon*; Manchester Evening News Award 1990 for *The Marriage of Figaro*. Dominic was Associate Director of the Royal Court 1999–2002 and Associate Director of the RSC 2002–2006, and is currently the Artistic Director of the Royal Court.

Other Adaptations in this Series

ANIMAL FARM
Ian Wooldridge
Adapted from George Orwell

ANNA KARENINA
Helen Edmundson
Adapted from Leo Tolstoy

ARTHUR & GEORGE
David Edgar
Adapted from Julian Barnes

THE CANTERBURY TALES
Mike Poulton
Adapted from Geoffrey Chaucer

A CHRISTMAS CAROL
Karen Louise Hebden
Adapted from Charles Dickens

CORAM BOY
Helen Edmundson
Adapted from Jamila Gavin

DAVID COPPERFIELD
Alastair Cording
Adapted from Charles Dickens

DR JEKYLL AND MR HYDE
David Edgar
Adapted from Robert Louis Stevenson

DRACULA
Liz Lochhead
Adapted from Bram Stoker

EMMA
Martin Millar and Doon MacKichan
Adapted from Jane Austen

FAR FROM THE MADDING CROWD
Mark Healy
Adapted from Thomas Hardy

FAUSTUS
Rupert Goold and Ben Power
After Christopher Marlowe

FRANKENSTEIN
Patrick Sandford
Adapted from Mary Shelley

GREAT EXPECTATIONS
Nick Ormerod and Declan Donnellan
Adapted from Charles Dickens

HIS DARK MATERIALS
Nicholas Wright
Adapted from Philip Pullman

JANE EYRE
Polly Teale
Adapted from Charlotte Brontë

THE JUNGLE BOOK
Stuart Paterson
Adapted from Rudyard Kipling

KES
Lawrence Till
Adapted from Barry Hines

MADAME BOVARY
Fay Weldon
Adapted from Gustave Flaubert

MARY BARTON
Rona Munro
Adapted from Elizabeth Gaskell

THE MILL ON THE FLOSS
Helen Edmundson
Adapted from George Eliot

MORTE D'ARTHUR
Mike Poulton
After Thomas Malory

NORTHANGER ABBEY
Tim Luscombe
Adapted from Jane Austen

NOUGHTS & CROSSES
Dominic Cooke
Adapted from Malorie Blackman

PERSUASION
Mark Healy
Adapted from Jane Austen

THE RAGGED TROUSERED
    PHILANTHROPISTS
Howard Brenton
Adapted from Robert Tressell

THE RAILWAY CHILDREN
Mike Kenny
Adapted from E. Nesbit

SENSE AND SENSIBILITY
Mark Healy
Adapted from Jane Austen

SLEEPING BEAUTY
Rufus Norris

SUNSET SONG
Alastair Cording
Adapted from Lewis Grassic Gibbon

TREASURE ISLAND
Stuart Paterson
Adapted from Robert Louis Stevenson

WAR AND PEACE
Helen Edmundson
Adapted from Leo Tolstoy

ARABIAN NIGHTS

adapted by

DOMINIC COOKE

NICK HERN BOOKS

London

www.nickhernbooks.co.uk

A Nick Hern Book

This edition of *Arabian Nights* first published in Great Britain in 2009 as a paperback original by Nick Hern Books Limited, The Glasshouse, 49a Goldhawk Road, London W12 8QP

Reprinted 2011 (twice), 2012

Published in an earlier version in 1998

Arabian Nights copyright © 2009 Dominic Cooke

Dominic Cooke has asserted his right to be identified as the author of this work

Cover illustration by Nomoco at Poco
Cover typography by RSC Graphic Design
Cover design by Ned Hoste, 2H

Typeset by Nick Hern Books, London
Printed and bound in Great Britain by Mimeo Ltd, Huntingdon, Cambridgeshire PE29 6XX

A CIP catalogue record for this book is available from the British Library

ISBN   978 1 84842 058 8

MIX
Paper from
responsible sources
FSC® C019549
FSC
www.fsc.org

This adaptation of *Arabian Nights* was first performed at the Young Vic on 16 November 1998. A new production was performed by the Royal Shakespeare Company at The Courtyard Theatre, Stratford-Upon-Avon, on 5 December 2009, with the following cast:

Nathalie Armin
Paul Bhattacharjee
Silas Carson
Daniel Cerqueira
Natalie Dew
Ayesha Dharker
Marcus Fernando
Kiran Landa
Jane Leaney
Kevork Malikyan
Adura Onashile
Chetna Pandya
Chris Ryman
Amit Shah
Nav Sidhu
Simon Trinder
Harvey Virdi
Rene Zagger

Director	Dominic Cooke
Designer	Georgia McGuinness
Lighting Designer	Hugh Vanstone
Sound Designer	Paul Arditti
Composer	Gary Yershon
Movement Director	Liz Ranken

For Aoife

4

Characters

THE STORY OF ES-SINDIBAD THE SAILOR
PORTER
PAGE
ES-SINDIBAD
MERCHANT
MERCHANT 2
MERCHANT 3

HOW ABU HASSAN BROKE WIND
ABU HASSAN
MARRIAGE BROKER
UNCLE
AUNT
PREACHER
FAKIR
FRIEND
FOE
BRIDE
GIRL
MOTHER

THE STORY OF THE WIFE WHO WOULDN'T EAT
HAROUN AL-RASHID
SIDI 1
SIDI 2
AMINA
GHOUL
BAKER
CUSTOMER 1
CUSTOMER 2
SORCERESS

THE STORY OF THE ENVIOUS SISTERS
KING
KING'S VIZIER
ELDEST SISTER
SECOND SISTER
YOUNGEST SISTER
BAHMAN
STEWARD
STEWARD'S WIFE
PERVIZ
PARIZADE
WOMAN
DERVISH
STONES
TALKING BIRD
HEAD COOK

Also various extras

Note on the text

There should be no blackouts. The action of the play should be continuous.

Note on the setting

An empty space with two areas: one for storytelling and one for listening.

Note on the cast

The original production called for a company of nine. The parts
could happily be played by the same or more actors and
distributed differently. It is essential that Shahrayar is listening,
and not participating in the first few stories, and preferable that
there is some resonance between the casting of 'The Story of the
Envious Sisters' and the frame story. Suggested doubling for a
company of nine could be:

Shahrayar / Ghoul / King (in 'The Story of the Envious Sisters')

Vizier / Captain / Doctor / Es-Sindibad / Haroun Al-Rashid /
King's Vizier

Slave / Ali Baba / Beggar / Sidi 2 / Baker / Perviz

Headsman / Baba Mustapha / Steward (in 'The Story of the Little
Beggar) / Abu Hassan / Steward (in 'The Story of the Envious
Sisters')

Kasim / Ali Baba's Son / Tailor / Watchman / Porter / Sidi 1 /
Head Cook / Bahman

Shahrazad / Chief of Police / Sorceress / Youngest Sister /
Talking Bird

Dinarzad / Kasim's Wife / Tailor's Wife / Hangman / Page /
Customer 2 / Parizade

Ali's Wife / Doctor's Wife / King (in 'The Story of the Little
Beggar') / Customer 1 / Second Sister

Queen / Marjanah / Merchant (in 'The Story of the Little
Beggar') / Amina / Eldest Sister

8

Prologue

SHAHRAZAD. Long long ago, in a faraway land, there lived a clever young girl called Shahrazad.

DINARZAD. She lived with her little sister who was called Dinarzad...

VIZIER. and her father, who was the Vizier, the Chief Adviser to the King.

The Vizier loved both his daughters very much.

A family grouping.

DINARZAD. Dinarzad was as kind, loyal and true as any girl her age...

SHAHRAZAD. but Shahrazad was courageous, shrewd and bright, well beyond her years.

And there was nothing she liked better than to read stories.

DINARZAD. Stories of enchanted caves...

SHAHRAZAD. flesh-eating ghouls...

DINARZAD. talking birds...

SHAHRAZAD. flying men.

DINARZAD. And night after night, Shahrazad would keep her little sister awake by filling her head with these stories.

DINARZAD *lies in bed with the covers pulled high.* SHAHRAZAD *sits at the end of the bed. She is in the middle of telling a terrifying story.*

SHAHRAZAD. When suddenly the huge bird dropped him in a valley of slimy tree-sized snakes.

DINARZAD *screams.*

VIZIER (*entering*). It's getting very late, children, you must get some sleep.

DINARZAD. Please, Father, please let Shahrazad finish.

SHAHRAZAD. We're near the end now.

VIZIER. Very well. The end of the story. Then bed.

SHAHRAZAD. However many times she told these stories, she never forgot a word, for Shahrazad was gifted with a perfect memory.

SHAHRAYAR. Now, the King of this country was called Shahrayar.

QUEEN. He lived with a beautiful wife that he loved as he loved his own eyes.

Another family grouping. They dance together, romantically.

SHAHRAYAR. Shahrayar was a great leader, courageous, big-hearted and strong. By his enemies he was feared, but by his people he was loved.

JESTER. And the halls of the Palace would sing with his laughter.

We see SHAHRAYAR *with his* JESTER. *The* JESTER *tumbles for* SHAHRAYAR. SHAHRAYAR *laughs. The* JESTER *tumbles off.*

SHAHRAYAR. One day, Shahrayar was at the Palace window overlooking the garden, when a secret door opened.

SHAHRAYAR *watches as his wife, the* QUEEN, *comes out. She looks around.*

QUEEN. Masud, Masud!

A SLAVE *jumps from a tree and rushes to her. They dance very sensually together. They exit.*

SHAHRAYAR. I trusted my wife as I trusted the ground beneath my feet. Curse life, curse the world and curse all women!

VIZIER. Now, the King is strengthened by his Vizier as the body is by the back.

SHAHRAYAR. Shahrayar went to the Vizier and said to him:

Take that wife of mine and put her to death.

VIZIER. The Vizier did this, for, if he disobeyed the King's will, he would be killed himself.

SHAHRAYAR. The gates of the King's heart were locked like a prison...

VIZIER. and the halls of the Palace were as silent as a tomb.

SHAHRAYAR. The King gave his word that, from now on, he would marry for just one night...

A stilted wedding dance.

and at sunrise the next morning...

VIZIER. he would order the Vizier to have the Headsman cut off his wife's head.

SHAHRAYAR. He continued to do this for a thousand nights...

SHAHRAYAR *pulls the petals off a red rose one by one.*

WOMEN. till a thousand young girls perished.

SHAHRAYAR. And every morning he would say to himself:

There is not a single good woman anywhere on the face of the earth.

SHAHRAZAD. By now, Shahrazad had grown up into a wise, refined and beautiful young woman.

DINARZAD. Dinarzad had grown up too!

VIZIER. One day, the Vizier returned home from the Palace with his head weighed down with worry.

The VIZIER *comes in as if from work. He kisses his daughters. They remove his scarf and hat.*

SHAHRAZAD. Why are you looking so lost, Father?

VIZIER. I'm just a little tired, that's all.

SHAHRAZAD. I hate to see you carrying the weight of the world on your shoulders.

VIZIER. I have devoted my life in service to the King and God.

SHAHRAZAD. But the King is not in service to God when he kills innocent young women.

VIZIER. The King is always in service to God. For God has chosen him to be King.

SHAHRAZAD. Even when he breaks God's law?

VIZIER. The law is whatever the King wills it to be.

SHAHRAZAD. Then the sun shall set on our city for ever.

Pause.

Father, I have a favour to ask and I hope that you will grant me it.

VIZIER. I will not refuse. If it is just and reasonable.

SHAHRAZAD. I have a plan to save the daughters of the city.

VIZIER. Your aim, daughter, is admirable. But King Shahrayar's sickness is beyond the help of any man. How could you hope to cure it?

SHAHRAZAD. I want you to marry me to the King.

Silence.

I want you to marry me to him today.

VIZIER. Is this your idea of a joke?

SHAHRAZAD. No.

VIZIER. You've been reading too many stories, my child.

SHAHRAZAD. Trust me, Father. Let me heal the King.

VIZIER. Silence. Or you shall go to your room. Dinarzad, tell your sister.

DINARZAD. I think she means it, Father.

SHAHRAZAD. Father, if I succeed I could save the lives of thousands.

If I die, I die an honourable death. Marry me to the King. Tonight.

VIZIER. And tomorrow?

SHAHRAZAD. I will face that when it comes.

VIZIER. The Headsman's blade is sharp. The ground of the Palace courtyard is stained red with blood. The sky above the Palace is spotted black with vultures.

SHAHRAZAD. There are some things more important than life, Father.

VIZIER. There is nothing more important than my daughter's life.

SHAHRAZAD. What about all those other daughters' lives, aren't they important too?

VIZIER. How dare you say that to me? I've thought about nothing else for months.

DINARZAD. On Friday, we were on our way to the mosque for noon prayers. By the Palace gates, we saw a mother pleading with the guards. She was clasping their ankles and kissing their feet, but they wouldn't listen. You should have heard her cries. It was awful.

VIZIER. I don't want you going out. You must pray at home from now on.

DINARZAD. And the marketplace was hissing with whispers. I saw one man. Red with rage, he was. 'Blood must flow for the life of my daughter,' he was saying. 'Death to the King.'

VIZIER. God spare us.

He gets up to go. She kneels at his feet.

SHAHRAZAD. I'm begging you, Father, and I will never stop begging until you do as I ask. As sure as moon follows sun and sun follows moon, I will beg and beg until you marry me to the King.

VIZIER. I will never marry you to the King.

SHAHRAZAD. Very well, you leave me no choice. If you don't marry me to the King tonight, I shall go to him myself.

VIZIER. Silence!

SHAHRAZAD. And I will tell the King that I asked you to marry me to him and you refused. That you begrudged him your daughter and disobeyed his will.

VIZIER. Who are you? Are you my daughter?

SHAHRAZAD. Yes. The daughter you instructed to serve God the merciful, in all her thoughts and deeds. The daughter you encouraged to put others before herself.

VIZIER. The daughter who I taught to respect and obey her father.

He goes to leave.

SHAHRAZAD. Stop, Father. Look at me.

He does.

I will go to the King, but you will never have to take me to the Headsman. I promise. I swear in the name of God Himself.

VIZIER. They all think they'll be saved. You're not the first.

SHAHRAZAD. Have I ever lied to you? Have I ever broken my word? Or made a promise I couldn't keep? Have I ever been unrealistic or overreached myself?

Pause.

Father, have I?

Pause.

Well, have I?

VIZIER. You are a child.

SHAHRAZAD. I am your daughter and I will honour you until the seas dry up. I will love you till the stars fall out of the sky, till the world itself dries up and turns to dust, but I have my own destiny that has been shaped by God and I have to be allowed to follow it. According to God's plan. To God's law. And there is no law higher than that. Not that of a king. Not even that of a father.

VIZIER. The Vizier went to King Shahrayar.

SHAHRAYAR. Vizier, do you love your daughter?

VIZIER. I love her as the thirsty traveller loves the oasis. As the fish loves the sea and the owl loves the night. She and her sister are the very air I breathe.

SHAHRAYAR. And yet you are prepared to marry her to her death?

Pause.

You realise that I cannot make any exceptions. For I have given my word. And a king's word is as precious as water.

VIZIER. My King and Lord, I have explained this to her, but she insists on being with you tonight.

SHAHRAYAR. With all respect, Vizier, she must be either a shrew or a halfwit.

VIZIER. She's neither, My Lord. Just very determined.

SHAHRAYAR. And what about you, Vizier? Do you really have the courage, the heartlessness to give her to the Headsman tomorrow?

VIZIER. There are some things more important than human life, Your Majesty.

SHAHRAYAR. Such as?

VIZIER. Loyalty, honour, service.

SHAHRAYAR. Go to her, prepare her and bring her to me at nightfall.

VIZIER. I am and I will always be your humble servant, My Lord.

SHAHRAYAR. Very good, Vizier.

VIZIER. The Vizier returned home and told his daughter the King's will.

SHAHRAZAD. Shahrazad went to her younger sister.

Now, Dinarzad, listen closely to what I have to say. When I go to the King, I will send for you to stay with me in the bridal chamber. When you come, remember to wake me an hour before daybreak and ask me to tell you a story.

DINARZAD. Sister, I will do all I can to help you.

VIZIER. At nightfall, the Vizier led Shahrazad to the Palace of great King Shahrayar.

The VIZIER *kisses* SHAHRAZAD.

May Heaven not deprive me of you.

The VIZIER *presents* SHAHRAZAD *to* SHAHRAYAR.

SHAHRAZAD *kisses the ground beneath* SHAHRAYAR. *The* VIZIER *goes.*

A short, strained, ritual wedding dance.

SHAHRAYAR. Uncover your face.

SHAHRAZAD *removes her veil.*

You are very beautiful.

SHAHRAZAD *starts crying.*

Why are you crying?

SHAHRAZAD. I have a sister. I would like her to stay with me here tonight, so that I might say goodbye and enjoy her company one last time.

SHAHRAYAR. Shahrayar agreed and Dinarzad was sent for…

DINARZAD. who came with all possible speed.

SHAHRAYAR. The King and Queen got into a bed raised very high…

DINARZAD. and Dinarzad lay down on some cushions on the floor underneath.

An hour before daybreak, Dinarzad did as her sister asked.

DINARZAD *clears her throat.*

Sister, if you are not too sleepy, tell me one of your strange and wonderful stories to wile away the night. For I don't know what will happen to you tomorrow.

SHAHRAZAD. May I have permission to tell a story, My Lord?

SHAHRAYAR. You may.

SHAHRAZAD. Very well.

Listen…

16

ACT ONE

The Story of Ali Baba and the Forty Thieves

In this story, the THIEVES *are played as a chorus, becoming the horses, the cave, and the treasure inside.*

SHAHRAZAD. In a city in Persia, there lived two brothers, one called Kasim and the other Ali Baba. When their father died he left them an equal share of the little he had, but fortune was not half as fair. Kasim married a widow who owned a shop bursting with fine goods. He soon became a wealthy man and lived a life of ease. Ali Baba, on the other hand, married a woman as dirt poor as he was. He lived very sparsely and was forced to scratch a living chopping wood in a nearby forest. Day after day he'd chop and chip and hack and split, until his back ached and his hands blistered and the sun was so low in the sky that he could barely see the blade of his axe. Then he'd bring the wood home to sell the next day on two skinny donkeys, which were all he owned in the world.

ALI BABA. One day, when Ali Baba was in the forest, he noticed, in the distance, a vast cloud of dust. When he peered closer he saw a band of horsemen riding towards him at great speed. Ali Baba was suspicious. He tied his donkeys behind a nearby bush and clambered up a tall, close-leafed tree next to a cliff, where he could see without being seen.

The THIEVES *enter. They are wearing black capes, armed with knives and carrying bulging saddlebags.* SHAHRAZAD *joins them.*

CAPTAIN. Dismount!

The THIEVES *dismount.*

ALI BABA. Ali Baba counted the men and found that they numbered forty. From their dead eyes and shining daggers he guessed that they were bandits.

CAPTAIN. The one he took for their Captain passed under the tree and stood in front of the cliff.

The THIEVES *become the cliff.*

OPEN SESAME!

The 'cliff door' opens. CAPTAIN *enters and also becomes the cliff.*

ALI BABA. Immediately, the door swept shut.

The door shuts.

Ali Baba froze in the tree like a falcon fixed on its prey. Eventually, the door opened again, and the Forty Thieves appeared.

CAPTAIN. CLOSE SESAME!

The door shuts.

SHAHRAZAD. Each thief mounted his horse and they galloped off into the dust.

ALI BABA *climbs down and goes to the door.*

ALI BABA. OPEN SESAME.

Instantly the door flies wide open. The THIEVES *become the inside of the cliff by reversing their capes which are lined with gold.*

Ali Baba was astonished to find a bright, airy cavern, carved out of the rock like the holy dome of a mosque. Inside was a landscape of limitless riches. Islands of sparkling treasure sat in rivers of rich silks and brocades, valleys of precious carpets and, above all, mountain upon mountain of sacks and purses bursting with shimmering gold and silver coins. He realised that this cavern had been a hiding place, not for years but for centuries, for generation after generation of thieves.

He quickly scooped up as many gold coins as his donkeys could bear.

OPEN SESAME!

He exits the cave.

CLOSE SESAME!

At once the door shuts.

He disguised the coins with firewood to prevent them from being seen and set off for home.

Wife, look at this.

He puts the bags at her feet. ALI'S WIFE *prods them, looks inside one. Then he empties the bags on to the floor, and the cascades of gold dazzle her eyes.*

ALI'S WIFE. Oh, Ali Baba, what have you done? We may be poor but that doesn't mean you have the right to steal. If you get caught, they'll cut off your hand. If they cut off your hand, you can't chop wood. If you can't chop wood, we'll have no money. If we have no money, we have no food. If we have no food, we'll starve. If we starve, we'll...

ALI BABA. Wife –

ALI'S WIFE. You've brought shame upon this house! You've lied, you've stolen! You've ruined everything!

ALI'S WIFE *starts hitting her husband with her fists under the following lines:*

How could you? How could you? How –

ALI BABA. Calm down and keep quiet. Wait till you hear what just happened.

He told her his adventures from beginning to end and they agreed to keep the whole story as secret as the mystery of the Sphinx.

ALI'S WIFE (*screaming*). We're rich!

ALI BABA. Shhh!

She does a little dance of joy and then starts to count the gold, piece by piece.

ALI'S WIFE. One, two, three, four...

ALI BABA. Don't be a dolt, wife. It would take all week to get this lot counted. We need to hide the coins right now. I'll dig a hole in the garden.

ALI'S WIFE. No, it's no good. I simply have to know how big our fortune is. I know. I'll borrow some scales from your brother. I'll quickly weigh the gold while you dig the hole.

ALI BABA. If you insist. But remember: he who is silent is safe.

ALI'S WIFE. Ali Baba's wife fluttered over to her brother-in-law Kasim, who lived nearby. As he was not at home, she asked his wife if she would kindly lend her some scales for a short while.

KASIM'S WIFE. Certainly. Wait here while I fetch them.

Now, the sister-in-law knew that Ali Baba was as poor as a pebble, and immediately smelt a rat. 'They can barely afford a bowl of rice between the three of them,' she thought, 'What the devil could they have enough of that it needs to be weighed?' So in order to catch them out, she greased the inside of the pan of the scales.

KASIM'S WIFE *goes back and gives the scales to* ALI'S WIFE.

I am sorry it's taken me so long, my dear. The servants had mislaid them.

ALI'S WIFE. Ali Baba's wife rushed the scales home and began to weigh the gold. Then, whilst Ali Baba buried it, she returned the scales, saying:

Sister-in-law, I said I would only be a while. I am as good as my word. Here they are. I am much obliged.

ALI'S WIFE *turns to leave.* KASIM'S WIFE *peers into the scales and finds a piece of gold stuck to the pan.*

KASIM'S WIFE. What's this? Ali Baba has enough gold coins to fill a pair of scales? Where did the penniless pauper get it from?

Kasim's wife couldn't wait to tell her husband the news, but she had to button her lip till he returned from his shop that evening.

Enter KASIM.

Kasim, you think yourself a wealthy man, but you are mistaken. Ali Baba has far more money than you. He doesn't count his gold as you do, he weighs it.

KASIM'S WIFE *shows* KASIM *the gold coin. He bites it. It's real.*

KASIM. Instead of feeling happy for his brother's good fortune, Kasim was stricken with deadly jealousy and didn't sleep a wink all night. Before sunrise the next morning, he marched straight over to his brother's house.

KASIM *knocks on* ALI BABA*'s door.*

Ali Baba, my wife found this stuck to the scales you borrowed yesterday.

KASIM *shows* ALI BABA *the coin.*

I demand an explanation.

ALI BABA. Ali Baba realised that, thanks to his dizzy wife, Kasim had discovered their secret. So rather than risking all the thieves' gold, he struck a deal. He agreed to tell Kasim where he found the treasure, if Kasim would share it equally and promise never to tell a soul.

KASIM. Determined to get the treasure first, at dawn the next day, Kasim set off with wooden chests loaded onto ten mules.

Enter the THIEVES *as mules.*

He followed the directions Ali Baba had given him, till he reached the cliff.

The THIEVES *become the cliff.*

OPEN SESAME!

The door flies open. As he enters, the THIEVES *become the inside of the cave.*

His eyes pored over the riches inside, which were beyond his wildest dreams. Greed and longing so possessed him that he spent the day in open-mouthed wonder, and clean forgot till evening that he had come to take some of the treasure away.

At last he snapped out of his trance and dragged as many sacks as he could to the door.

OPEN SEMOLINA!

The door remains closed.

OPEN SULTANA!... OPEN SUNFLOWER!... OPEN SARDINE!

The stubborn door doesn't budge.

The more Kasim searched for the word, the more it escaped him, until the fire of his greed was extinguished by waves of icy dread.

SHAHRAZAD. At nightfall, the thieves returned to their cavern and noticed Kasim's mules grazing sleepily by the rock, loaded with empty trunks.

The CAPTAIN *sends some* THIEVES *to look for an intruder.*

CAPTAIN. The Captain marched straight to the door, his steely dagger glinting in his hand.

OPEN SESAME!

KASIM *charges towards the door, the* THIEVES *surround him and kill him.*

SHAHRAZAD. The thieves resolved to cut Kasim's body into quarters and display it inside the cavern, hanging two pieces on one side of the door and two on the other. This would scare off anyone else who attempted to break in. Then, they mounted their horses, and set off to search the countryside for caravans to rob.

The THIEVES *disappear.*

KASIM'S WIFE. Brother-in-law, please help me! It's late and my husband hasn't come back from the forest and I'm terrified something dreadful has happened.

ALI BABA. Sister-in-law, you must stay calm. I'm sure Kasim thought it wise not to return to the city till late at night for fear of being seen.

KASIM'S WIFE. Maybe you're right. He did tell me it was important to carry out his mission secretly.

ALI BABA. Absolutely, you go home and wait for him. And above all, stay calm. I'm sure he'll come back soon.

KASIM'S WIFE. Kasim's wife returned home and waited patiently till midnight. At this point she became truly petrified and cursed herself for her ill-judged curiosity and dimwitted desire to meddle in her sister-in-law's affairs. She spent the whole night in anguish and at daybreak she ran back to Ali Baba's, where her arrival was announced not by her words but by her tears.

ALI BABA. Immediately, Ali Baba set off for the forest with his donkeys. When he approached the cliff, he saw no sign of Kasim or his mules. But he did see a pool of blood by the door which chilled him to the bone. He crept to the door and gave the command.

OPEN SESAME!

ALI BABA *finds the quartered body.*

Despite Kasim's coldness towards him, Ali Baba knew that, according to the religious law of his land, his brother must be buried whole. So without hesitating, he found a cloth to wrap up the remains. Then, he loaded them on to his donkeys, with three more sacks of gold, and set off back to his brother's house in town, taking care to wait at the forest's edge until nightfall to avoid being seen.

ALI BABA *knocks at the door.*

MARJANAH. The door was opened by Marjanah, a clever slave-girl.

ALI BABA. Marjanah, my life depends on your secrecy.

MARJANAH. What's happened?

ALI BABA. These two bundles contain your master's murdered body.

MARJANAH. Merciful Heavens!

ALI BABA. Without raising any suspicion, we must find a way to bury him whole and as if he died of natural causes. For if talk gets round that he was murdered, his killers will come in search of me as his accomplice.

MARJANAH. Leave it to me.

ALI BABA. Remember: he who is silent is safe.

MARJANAH. What shall we tell my mistress?

ALI BABA. Leave that to me.

MARJANAH. The following morning, Marjanah went to a nearby Druggist and asked him for tablets that would treat a deadly disease.

DRUGGIST. The Druggist gave her a small bottle and enquired:

Who is ill?

MARJANAH (*tearfully*). Ah. It is Kasim himself, my master. We don't know what it is, but he hasn't spoken a word or eaten a crumb for days. Keep it to yourself, but it's not looking good, I'm afraid.

SHAHRAZAD. By early evening, word had spread around the city that Kasim was on his last legs. And, as neighbours watched Ali Baba and his wife entering the house with sad, downcast eyes, they were not surprised to hear the heartrending cries of Kasim's wife and Marjanah...

MARJANAH. who announced that Kasim was dead.

First thing the next morning, Marjanah set off to visit a poor old cobbler on the market square called Baba Mustapha.

BABA. Because he was so penniless, he needed to work harder than anyone else and his shop was always the first to open.

MARJANAH. Good morning.

She offers BABA MUSTAPHA *a gold coin.*

Baba Mustapha, fetch your needle and thread and come with me quickly. But I must warn you, when we leave the town centre, I shall blindfold you.

BABA. What the devil are you up to, Marjanah? I don't like the sound of this. I've got my reputation to think about.

MARJANAH *offers another gold coin. He doesn't accept.*

MARJANAH. Your good name is safe in my hands. Come with me quickly and fear nothing.

BABA MUSTAPHA *pockets the coins.*

BABA. Baba Mustapha followed Marjanah through the early morning shadows, to the edge of the town centre.

She blindfolds him.

MARJANAH. She blindfolded him and led him to Kasim's house and into the room where the quartered body lay.

She takes his blindfold off.

BABA. What a sight!

MARJANAH. Baba Mustapha, I brought you here to sew the pieces of this body together.

BABA. I knew you were up to no good.

MARJANAH. When you finish, I shall give you another piece of gold.

BABA MUSTAPHA *sews the four pieces into one.* MAR-JANAH *gives* BABA MUSTAPHA *another coin.*

She then blindfolds him again.

Marjanah led Baba Mustapha back to the edge of the town centre. Then she forced him to swear an oath of secrecy.

She takes the blindfold off.

He who is silent is safe.

When she returned, they carried Kasim's body to the cemetery.

SHAHRAZAD. And so the secret of Kasim's gruesome murder was locked away as tight as the clasp on a miser's purse. And no one in the city suspected a thing.

ALI BABA. Three days later, under the cloak of nightfall, Ali Baba...

ALI'S WIFE. his wife...

ALI'S SON. and their son...

ALI BABA. carried their few belongings...

ALI'S WIFE. with their gold...

ALI'S SON. to Kasim's big house...

ALI, ALI'S WIFE *and* ALI'S SON. to live in wealth and splendour.

ALI BABA. Ali Baba gave Kasim's thriving shop to his son...

ALI *gives his* SON *a key.*

promising that if he managed it wisely, he'd receive the key to greater riches when he married.

SHAHRAZAD. Let us leave Ali Baba to the fruits of his golden fortune and return to the Forty Thieves. When they returned to their forest hideaway, they were astonished to find Kasim's body and several bags of gold missing.

CAPTAIN. Someone else knows the secret of the cave! We must act without hesitation or everything that we and our ancestors have sweated blood for will be lost. I shall go down into the town and listen out for talk of a murdered man. I will find out who he was and where he lived. And when I track down his accomplice, we will put him to a slow and lingering death.

Temptation

SHAHRAYAR's *room. Dawn.*

Sound of a sword being sharpened.

Enter the VIZIER *and the* HEADSMAN.

VIZIER. Darkness bleeds into day, My Lord. The Headsman awaits your command.

DINARZAD. What an extraordinary story, Sister. I would love to hear the rest of it.

SHAHRAZAD. You will never guess what happens next. I shall tell you tonight, if the King lets me live.

VIZIER. Your Majesty?

SHAHRAZAD. Doesn't His Majesty want to know what happens next to Ali Baba?

Pause.

Or whether the cunning slave-girl outwits the Captain of the Forty Thieves?

Pause. SHAHRAYAR *is torn.*

SHAHRAYAR. Vizier, come back tomorrow. At the same time.

VIZIER. Certainly, Your Majesty.

SHAHRAZAD, DINARZAD *and the* VIZIER *make eye contact.*

Exit the VIZIER *and the* HEADSMAN.

SHAHRAZAD. The day melted into night.

DINARZAD. And an hour before daybreak, Dinarzad said:

Sister, if you are not too sleepy, tell the rest of your strange and wonderful story.

SHAHRAZAD. May I have your permission to continue the story, My Lord?

SHAHRAYAR. Yes.

SHAHRAZAD. Very well.

Listen…

The Story of Ali Baba and the Forty Thieves continues

SHAHRAZAD. The Captain of the Forty Thieves disguised himself and set off, arriving in the city at daybreak.

SHAHRAZAD *and* CAPTAIN. He walked and walked…

CAPTAIN. until he came to the first shop he saw open.

SHAHRAZAD. Guess what?

BABA. It was the shabby shop of Baba Mustapha.

BABA MUSTAPHA *sits with a needle in his hand, sewing a shoe.*

CAPTAIN. Good morning, old man. I'm surprised to see you working this early. There's barely enough light in the sky for you to do your sewing. Is it possible that at your fine old age you have such good eyesight?

BABA. You clearly don't know Baba Mustapha. I may be as old as the crumbling earth, but I still have perfect vision. Not long ago, in a place much darker than this, I stitched up the body of a dead man.

CAPTAIN. Really? A dead man? Why would you want to do that?

BABA. Ah. You want me to speak, but you shall know no more.

The CAPTAIN *pulls out a gold coin, and holds it out towards* BABA MUSTAPHA, *who is tempted but doesn't take it.*

He who is silent is safe.

CAPTAIN. Show me the dead man's house.

BABA. Even if I wanted to, I couldn't. I was blindfold. I didn't see a thing.

CAPTAIN. Come on, let me blindfold you again. We'll see if you can retrace your steps.

The CAPTAIN *takes out a second coin and holds that out as well. Silence. He takes out a third.* BABA MUSTAPHA *takes all three and swiftly pockets them.*

To the great joy of the Captain of the Forty Thieves…

BABA. Baba Mustapha stood up and led the Captain to the spot where Marjanah had bound his eyes.

The CAPTAIN *blindfolds* BABA MUSTAPHA.

BABA MUSTAPHA *leads off, retracing his steps.*

Then, step by step, alley by alley, he weaved his way back to Kasim's house, where Ali Baba now lived.

CAPTAIN. The Captain sent the old man on his way and, taking careful note of the location of the house, raced back to the forest. There, he ordered the thieves to buy twenty mules and forty large leather jars, one full of oil and the others completely empty. Firstly, he instructed each thief to grind their daggers as sharp as tigers' teeth. Then he told them to load two jars onto each mule and to each climb inside a jar. When this was done, he set off for town, arriving just as twilight shadows fell on Ali Baba's doorstep…

The CAPTAIN *puts on his oil-merchant disguise. The*
THIEVES *'climb inside jars' by wrapping themselves in their*
capes which are now lined with leather.

ALI BABA. where the owner was taking in some fresh evening
air…

ALI'S SON. with his son.

CAPTAIN. Sir, my name is Kawaja Hussain. I have brought
some oil from a faraway place to sell at market tomorrow.
Would it be possible to spend the night under your roof?

ALI BABA. Ali Baba didn't recognise the Captain through his
disguise.

My home is your home, my friend. Welcome.

He opens the gate to allow the mules into the yard.

CAPTAIN. Kawaja Hussain, or rather the Captain of the Forty
Thieves, unloaded the jars. He crept from jar to jar, saying:

Have your daggers at the ready. When the time is right I shall
return and give the signal.

After this, he slipped into the house, to join Ali Baba for
supper.

MARJANAH. Marjanah set about preparing a delicious meal.
While she was cooking, the oil lamp in the kitchen went out.
There were no candles or oil to be found in the house so she
picked up the oil pot and went into the yard to borrow some
from one of the leather jars. When she drew close to the first
jar…

SHAHRAZAD (*inside one of the jars*). the thief inside whispered: 'Is it time yet?'

MARJANAH. Any other slave but Marjanah would have bleated
like a goat, but she was too clever for that. Without so much
as a twitch she replied:

Not yet. But soon.

Jar by jar she tiptoed round, giving the same answer, until she
came to the jar filled with oil.

This way, Marjanah learned that there were forty vengeful thieves in the house and that this so-called oil merchant was their Captain.

She took the oil she needed and raced back to the kitchen. The second she lit the lamp, she grabbed the biggest pan she could find and sneaked back to the courtyard, where she filled it to the brim with thick, gloopy oil. Rushing into the kitchen, she set the pan onto a crackling fire. As soon as it bubbled and spat, she picked up the pan and took it out into the courtyard.

MARJANAH *kills the* THIEVES *in their jars*.

Then she went to serve the food and wine.

The CAPTAIN, ALI BABA *and* ALI'S SON *eat and drink*.

CAPTAIN. Meanwhile, the Captain hatched a bloodthirsty scheme.

There's no need to call my men, he thought. It will give me great pleasure to deal with this cockroach myself. I shall get them both drunk so they fall asleep. Then, I shall slice my enemy in two like a ripe watermelon.

MARJANAH. However, Marjanah had spotted the Captain of the Forty Thieves' knife through his clothes and knew what he was up to.

She put on her dancer's veil.

MARJANAH *bows deeply*.

ALI BABA. Come in, Marjanah. Kawaja Hussein will tell us what he thinks of your performance.

MARJANAH. It gives me great pleasure to present the Dance of the Deadly Dagger.

MARJANAH *presents a dagger and performs a hugely ener-getic, mesmerising, sensual, sometimes violent dance in which she alternates between thrusting the dagger outwards as if to stab someone, and inwards as if to stab herself in the chest. Eventually,* MARJANAH *kills the* CAPTAIN.

ALI BABA. Wretched woman, what have you done? You've ruined us all.

MARJANAH. I did this to save you, not ruin you. See what an enemy you had within your gates. Look closely and you shall recognise the Captain of the Forty Thieves.

Marjanah told Ali Baba all that she had done.

ALI BABA. And Ali Baba showered her with thanks.

To show my appreciation, I give you your freedom from this moment and, if he will agree, my son's hand in marriage.

ALI'S SON. Far from refusing, his son was delighted.

MARJANAH. And a few days later...

ALI'S SON. with a sacred blessing and an extravagant feast...

ALI'S SON *and* MARJANAH. they were married.

Short wedding tableau that echoes that of SHAHRAYAR *and* SHAHRAZAD, *except this time full of joy and light. Just as the married couple kiss,* SHAHRAYAR *interrupts and the characters freeze.*

Threat

SHAHRAYAR*'s room. Dawn.*

Sound of a sword being sharpened.

SHAHRAYAR. So you think he was happy? This son of Ali Baba?

SHAHRAZAD. So the story goes.

SHAHRAYAR. He marries a crafty, cunning woman. He is sure to be tricked and lied to and crushed by this scheming slave-girl.

SHAHRAZAD. Your Majesty, the story says otherwise.

SHAHRAYAR. Your story is written by a liar!

Enter the VIZIER.

VIZIER. The Headsman is waiting outside, Your Majesty.

DINARZAD. I know you have many other tales, Sister. Perhaps you could tell us one tonight.

SHAHRAYAR. I have no more time to listen to your sister's prattling. Well, what are you waiting for, Vizier? Bring in the Headsman.

VIZIER. As you command, My Lord.

The VIZIER *exits.*

SHAHRAZAD. What a shame, Sister, for tonight I would have told you the intriguing tale of – Forgive me, Your Majesty, I speak out of turn.

SHAHRAYAR. Yes, you do.

SHAHRAZAD. I'm sorry, Your Majesty, I just can't contain my excitement when I think about this story. It's one of my favourites.

Once there lived a Tailor with...

Enter the VIZIER *and the* HEADSMAN. *The* HEADSMAN *approaches* SHAHRAZAD.

DINARZAD. No, Your Majesty, please, I beg you.

The HEADSMAN *grabs* SHAHRAZAD.

SHAHRAYAR. One word before you go. Woman, what is the name of the story you were going to tell?

SHAHRAZAD. 'The Story of the Little Beggar'.

SHAHRAYAR. What sort of story is it?

SHAHRAZAD. One to put a smile on a king's face.

SHAHRAYAR. Laughter died with my first wife.

SHAHRAZAD. The King in this story finds laughter where he least expects it.

SHAHRAYAR. I have a mind to hear it. Vizier, Headsman – tomorrow.

The VIZIER *signals to the* HEADSMAN *to release* SHAHRAZAD. SHAHRAZAD, DINARZAD *and the* VIZIER *catch each other's eyes.*

Exit the VIZIER *and the* HEADSMAN.

SHAHRAZAD. The day melted into night.

DINARZAD. And an hour before daybreak, Dinarzad said:

> Sister, if you are not too sleepy, tell us another strange and
> wonderful story.

SHAHRAZAD. May I tell my story, My Lord?

SHAHRAYAR. You may.

SHAHRAZAD. Very well.

> Listen…

The Story of the Little Beggar

SHAHRAZAD. Once there lived a Tailor, with a pretty and
faithful wife. One day while taking a walk, they bumped into
a jolly Little Beggar.

The BEGGAR *is smartly dressed with a scarf and a tall green
hat, improvising a slapstick death routine with singing and
tambourine. The routine involves dying several times in
increasingly elaborate ways. The* TAILOR *and* TAILOR'S
WIFE *laugh and clap.*

TAILOR. When they got close they could smell wine on his
breath and realised that he was roaring drunk.

The BEGGAR *puts his tambourine under his arm and claps
his hands in time with his song:*

BEGGAR.
> If you fancy a giggle,
> I'll cartwheel or I'll wiggle,
> And if I cheer you up,
> Empty your purse and fill my cup!

TAILOR'S WIFE. The Tailor and his wife took so strongly to
the Little Beggar that they asked him to come home with
them to eat.

TAILOR *and* TAILOR'S WIFE. They all sat down to a delicious
meal of bread and fish.

TAILOR. They ate and drank till they had finished everything...

TAILOR'S WIFE. except for one large fish.

TAILOR. I know. I bet you can't swallow this whole.

The BEGGAR *tries to swallow it.*

TAILOR *and* TAILOR'S WIFE. But a sharp piece of fishbone got stuck in his throat.

The BEGGAR *starts choking and falls to the floor. The* TAILOR *and* TAILOR'S WIFE *clap and laugh, thinking it is an act, till his body is still. They prod him. They check him. He is stone dead.*

Silence.

TAILOR'S WIFE. Don't just sit there. Do something.

TAILOR. What do you suggest?

TAILOR'S WIFE. You and your practical jokes! Ha-blooming-ha!

TAILOR. I wasn't to know he'd drop dead, was I?

TAILOR'S WIFE. Well, we'd better do something sharpish. Or we'll find ourselves hanged as murderers.

TAILOR. Oh my word.

TAILOR'S WIFE. Be quiet, I'm thinking... I know. Wrap him in a sheet, pick him up and follow me.

TAILOR. The Tailor did as his wife said...

TAILOR'S WIFE. And she led the way through the streets, wailing and shrieking:

My child, my child, I pray you be cured of this smallpox. Why you, my child, why you?

PASSERS-BY. And passers-by exclaimed:

Poor woman. Her child is ill with smallpox!

TAILOR *and* TAILOR'S WIFE. Soon they arrived at the house of a Doctor.

TAILOR. They climbed some steps to the front door.

TAILOR'S WIFE *knocks at the door.*

MAID. A maid answered.

TAILOR'S WIFE *hands the* MAID *a coin.*

TAILOR'S WIFE. Miss, please give this coin to your master.
Ask him to come to see my child who is gravely ill.

The MAID *goes to fetch the* DOCTOR.

They rest the body in the doorway.

MAID. Master, there is a gravely ill child downstairs with its
parents. They gave me a quarter piece of gold for you.

DOCTOR. Light, light, quickly, girl, quickly.

TAILOR'S WIFE. Put down the beggar and run!

DOCTOR. The Doctor rushed downstairs to the front door in the
dark. Not seeing the Little Beggar, he tripped over the body
and kicked it all the way down the steps.

The MAID *comes with a candle.*

MAID. Here's a candle, master.

DOCTOR. You dozy mare! Why didn't you bring it to me
earlier? Look what you made me do!

The DOCTOR *takes the candle and goes to the* BEGGAR. *He
takes the* BEGGAR's *arm and feels the pulse. Nothing.*

I am finished. I have killed the patient I was supposed to cure.
How will I get this body out of the house? If anyone sees me,
the word will get round and my reputation will be ruined. I'll
never work again. What can I do?

So, he carried the Little Beggar upstairs to his wife and told
her what happened.

DOCTOR'S WIFE. You're neither use nor ornament! What are
you standing there for with a face like a bottle of warts? It's
not your reputation you need to worry about, it's your life! If
the day breaks and he is still here, they will hang us as
murderers.

DOCTOR. What are we going to do?

DOCTOR'S WIFE. I know. We should drop him down the chimney of our next-door neighbour, the King's Steward. The cats and dogs often eat his larder clean of meat and butter. Perhaps they will eat up this body.

The DOCTOR *and* DOCTOR'S WIFE *take the* BEGGAR *up on the roof and drop him down the chimney. The* BEGGAR *lands on his feet. He stands, still wrapped in his blanket, bolt upright, leaning against a wall.*

STEWARD. Just then, the King's Steward came home.

He opens the door, with a candle in his hand, and sees the body.

What's this? A burglar? So it's not the cats and dogs who've been eating my meat and butter after all, it's a man. Well, I'll soon put a stop to that.

He picks up a stick and cracks it over the BEGGAR. *The* BEGGAR *falls. He gives him another blow on the back. He prods him. And again. Lifts up his eyelids and realises he is dead.*

Curses on my meat and butter. I've killed him! Heaven help me. What am I going to do?

He puts the BEGGAR *over his back.*

The Steward carried the Little Beggar to the marketplace and leaned him up against a shop.

Again, the BEGGAR *stands upright.*

MERCHANT. At that moment, a wealthy Merchant, the King's broker, staggered by in a drunken stupor.

The MERCHANT *stands against the wall next to – but without noticing – the* BEGGAR, *and urinates. In his drunkenness, he sways into the corpse, which falls onto the* MERCHANT's *back with arms round his neck.*

MERCHANT. Thief! Thief! Watchman! Help me!

The MERCHANT *throws the* BEGGAR *to the floor with a sharp blow and begins pummelling and choking him.*

WATCHMAN (*entering*). What is it? Get off that man immediately!

MERCHANT. It wasn't my fault, Watchman, he tried to rob me.

The WATCHMAN *checks the* BEGGAR *to see if he's breathing and listens to his chest.*

WATCHMAN. You've killed him. You're coming with me.

He grabs the MERCHANT *and ties him up.*

The Watchman took the Merchant to the Chief of Police…

CHIEF. who threw him in a cell and, next morning, went to tell the King.

KING. The King ordered the Merchant to be hanged…

CHIEF. and the Chief went to the Hangman…

HANGMAN. who set up a gallows and announced the execution.

Public execution. The MERCHANT *stands on a box. The* HANGMAN *places the noose around his neck. Drum roll.*

STEWARD *(from the audience)*. Stop. It wasn't the Merchant who killed the Little Beggar. It was me! It was me!

CHIEF. What did you say?

STEWARD. It was me! I killed the Little Beggar.

And the Steward told how he hit the Little Beggar with a stick and left him in the marketplace.

Don't hang him, hang me!

CHIEF. Release the Merchant and hang the Steward.

The HANGMAN *takes the noose off the* MERCHANT, *who steps down from the box. The* STEWARD *stands on the box. The* HANGMAN *places the noose around his neck. Drum roll.*

DOCTOR *(from the audience)*. Stop. It wasn't the Steward who killed the Little Beggar. It was me! It was me!

And the Doctor told how he had kicked the Little Beggar down the stairs and dropped him down the chimney of the Steward.

Don't hang him, hang me!

CHIEF. Release the Steward and hang the Doctor.

The HANGMAN *takes the noose off the* STEWARD, *who steps down from the box. The* DOCTOR *stands on the box. The* HANGMAN *places the noose around his neck. Drum roll.*

TAILOR (*from the audience*). Stop. It wasn't the Doctor who killed the Little Beggar. It was me! It was me!

And the Tailor told how he had choked the Little Beggar with a fishbone and left the body at the Doctor's house.

Don't hang him, hang me!

CHIEF. I've never heard the like. Release the Doctor and hang the Tailor.

The HANGMAN *starts to take the noose off the* DOCTOR, *who steps down from the box.*

DOCTOR. But –

CHIEF. Any more interruptions and I'll hang the lot of you.

DOCTOR. But –

CHIEF. WHAT IS IT?

DOCTOR. The Little Beggar is still breathing.

All turn to look at the BEGGAR*'s body. There is a strange choking sound. The* DOCTOR *opens his bag and takes out a giant pair of tweezers, opens the* BEGGAR*'s mouth and puts them down his throat, pulling out a huge fishbone.*

BEGGAR (*huge sneeze, stands bolt upright*).
　　　If you fancy a giggle,
　　　I'll cartwheel or I'll wiggle,
　　　And if I cheer you up,
　　　Empty your purse and fill my cup!

CHIEF. And word reached the King of the extraordinary story of the Little Beggar's death and the even more extraordinary story of his recovery.

KING. I've never heard a more extraordinary story in all my life.

And the King was so delighted with the story that he awarded robes of honour…

TAILOR. to the Tailor…

The TAILOR *steps forward to receive his robe.*

DOCTOR. Doctor…

The DOCTOR *steps forward to receive his robe.*

STEWARD. Steward…

The STEWARD *steps forward to receive his robe.*

MERCHANT. and Merchant…

The MERCHANT *steps forward to receive his robe.*

KING. and sent them on their way, thanking them for entertaining him with such an excellent story.

BEGGAR. The Little Beggar was appointed the King's jester…

SHAHRAZAD. and made the King chuckle for the rest of his days.

The KING *starts smiling, giggles, then a loud laugh cracks through him.*

Warning

SHAHRAYAR*'s room. Dawn.*

Sound of a sword being sharpened.

SHAHRAYAR. This laughing King is a fool like I once was. Before I learned the truth about women. Laughter should be a stranger to a king's heart.

Enter the VIZIER.

VIZIER. The darkness is lifting, My Lord. What shall I tell the Headsman?

DINARZAD. I would love to hear another of your wonderful stories tonight.

SHAHRAZAD. I will tell you one. An extraordinary tale of adventure and survival against all odds. If the King spares my life.

SHAHRAYAR. Do you take me for a fool, woman?

SHAHRAZAD. I know you to be the wisest of men, My Lord.

SHAHRAYAR. Then what makes you think you can trick me?

SHAHRAZAD. Trick you, Your Majesty?

SHAHRAYAR. Trying to tempt me with your senseless stories!

SHAHRAZAD. If you feel you are being tricked, good King, I shall never breathe a word of a story again.

SHAHRAYAR. I will be the one to decide that.

SHAHRAZAD. Yes, My Lord.

SHAHRAYAR. I hear your stories as and when I choose. And when I no longer choose, you will die like the others.

SHAHRAZAD. As Your Majesty pleases.

SHAHRAYAR. Vizier, you may go.

SHAHRAZAD, DINARZAD *and the* VIZIER *catch each other's eyes.*

Exit the VIZIER.

SHAHRAZAD. The day melted into night.

As day turns to night they go to bed.

Listen...

The Story of Es-Sindibad the Sailor

ES-SINDIBAD *uses a puppet of his younger self to act out much of his story. The rest of the images are created by the* COMPANY *using masks, models, objects and puppets.*

SHAHRAZAD. Once, in the city of Baghdad, there lived a poor man who earned his living by carrying things on his head. He was called Es-Sindibad the Porter.

One day, as he was staggering under a heavy load in the sweltering heat of the summer sun, he stopped to rest.

He found himself in a shaded spot by a fine Merchant's house.
A cool and fragrant breeze blew through the doorway, and
from within floated the sweet strains of a kamanja.

The PORTER *improvises the following song to the tune
coming from the house.*

PORTER (*singing*).
> Tell me, oh, tell me how it came to pass,
> Why some break their backs whilst some sit on their –
> Ask me, oh, ask me how can it be fair,
> That some lucky bleeders take more than their share?
>
> Many men sweat in the sun to get paid,
> While others they rest and recline in the shade.
>
> All God's creations live under one sun,
> Our bodies all equal, our souls all as one,
> Yet some men live poor lives, others live fine,
> One sips on vinegar, one guzzles wine.
>
> Many men sweat in the sun to get paid,
> While others they rest and recline in the shade.

He finishes the song and places his load on his head.

Just as he was about to go on his way...

PAGE. a smartly dressed Page appeared.

Please come in. My master would like to speak with you.

PORTER. The Porter politely declined...

PAGE. but the Page would not be deterred.

PORTER. So, Es-Sindibad left his load with the doorkeeper and
followed the Page into the house.

The space is filled with WEALTHY MERCHANTS *who are
eating, drinking and smoking hookahs. They are served by*
MALE SERVANTS *and* SLAVE-GIRLS.

He was led into a magnificent and spacious hall, as splendid
as the palace of a king. At one end sat a distinguished old man
whose beard was touched with silver.

The PORTER *kisses the ground before his host.*

ES-SINDIBAD. You are welcome, my friend. May this day bring you joy. What is your name and what do you do?

PORTER. My name is Es-Sindibad. By trade a porter.

ES-SINDIBAD. How strange! For my name is also Es-Sindibad. Es-Sindibad the Sailor. I heard your song.

PORTER. Please don't reproach me, sir. Poverty and hardship teach a man bad manners.

ES-SINDIBAD. Do not be ashamed, for you have become a brother to me. I found your song delightful.

Porter, I should like to tell you the story of how I came to sit where you see me now. For my wealth was not won without huge effort, much pain and grave, grave danger.

He indicates for the PORTER *to sit. The* PORTER *does so.*

Know this: my father was the owner of untold wealth and property. He died when I was a little boy and left it all to me. When I was a young man...

He produces a puppet of his younger self, which he uses to act out the rest of the story.

I ate and drank freely, wore fine clothes and frittered my days away chatting and joking with friends, as if my wealth would last for ever. By the time I came to my senses, I found that my money was spent and I was ruined.

Fear swallowed my heart. How on earth was I going to survive? In a trice, the answer came to me. I would see the world and not come back until I had made my fortune. So, I sold all my possessions, put my best foot forward and boarded a ship with a group of merchants bound for the golden city of El-Basrah.

One of the COMPANY *brings on the model of the ship, which encircles* ES-SINDIBAD *as in a memory or dream.*

We passed from island to island, from sea to sea, from country to country, and bought and sold and bargained until we came to a beautiful island. It was rich with leafy trees, mellow fruits, fragrant flowers, singing birds and crystal water. But there was not a soul to be seen.

I sat in the shade by a soothing stream. I ate my food and sipped on some wine. The air was heavy with the musk of wild flowers and before long I had drifted into a deep, deep sleep.

I cannot tell how long I slept, but when I woke up, the other passengers were gone. I raced frantically to the beach and looked out across the sea. There was the ship, a white speck in the vast blue ocean, dissolving into the distance. The ship had sailed with everyone on board, and no one had remembered me.

Broken with terror and despair, I collapsed upon the sand. I wailed. I beat my chest. I cursed myself a thousand times for leaving Baghdad. For I was all alone without a crumb to eat or a thing to my name. I thought I was going mad.

The puppet climbs a tree and gazes from left to right.

I scrambled up a tree. I gazed from left to right. All I could see was sky and water and trees and birds and islands and sand. But when I scanned the island more closely, I noticed, to my surprise, a strange, white dome looming in the distance.

The puppet approaches a huge white egg.

He explores the egg and tries to climb up.

He walks around, counting the circumference pace by pace.

I stood there puzzling over how to get inside, when suddenly the sky turned black.

A gigantic bird, also played by the COMPANY, *hovers over the puppet.*

In a flash I was reminded of a story I had once heard from an adventurer: on a faraway island there lives a bird of monstrous size called a Rukh, which feeds its young on elephants. Instantly, I realised that this dome was none other than a Rukh's egg.

The bird lands on the egg and falls asleep. The puppet creeps close and stands by one of its legs.

When the Rukh was fast asleep, I sprung into action.

The puppet uses his turban to tie himself to the bird's foot.

Praise be to God. This bird will carry me out of here. To civilisation.

Daybreak. The bird wakes up, screeches loudly and flies, carrying the puppet up to the sky, soaring higher and higher. It slowly swoops into land. When it does, the puppet escapes, and the bird flies away.

I found myself at the base of a valley as deep as dread, surrounded by mountains so high, they stabbed the clouds like spears. Why didn't I stay on the island? At least there was food and water there. Here there is nothing! I am a fool, an idiot, a blockhead!

I walked around the valley and was staggered to find that the ground was covered with priceless diamonds. The entire valley blazed in glorious light. To my horror, here and there amongst the shimmering stones were coils of deadly snakes, each large enough to swallow a camel.

The COMPANY *play snakes using glove puppets.*

As the sun came up, they were slithering back to their darkened dens, for, in daylight, they hid in fear of being carried away by Rukhs and eagles and eaten.

Consumed by terror and weak with hunger, I roamed the valley all day, searching for somewhere safe to spend the night.

When suddenly, something fell out of the sky and landed smack bang in front of me with a loud thud. It was a joint of lamb!

I was baffled, for there was not a soul in sight. Who or what could have thrown this meat? Quick as a wink, it came to me. I recalled a story I had once heard from travellers who had visited the Valley of the Diamonds. It is a place too dangerous to enter. But some crafty merchants had hit upon a wily scheme to gather jewels from the valley floor. At dawn, they would take a sheep, cut it up, and throw the pieces from the top of the mountain into the valley. The meat is fresh and moist and the diamonds stick to it. At midday, they wait until the eagles swoop down, pick up the meat and lift it away in their talons to their nests at the top of the mountain. With a mighty din, the merchants would rush at the birds. This would scare the eagles away, leaving the meat in the nest and diamonds for the merchants.

Till that moment I truly believed I would never leave this valley alive. But at a stroke, I started to see a way out.

Not wishing to waste the riches at my feet, I gathered as many of the biggest diamonds I could find. I stuffed my pockets, my clothes, even my shoes to bursting.

The puppet grabs the meat and lies underneath it.

An eagle enters, the puppet waves at it. It swoops down, grabs the meat between its talons and soars up into the air, with the puppet clinging on for dear life. The eagle lands in its nest. Enter another puppet, the MERCHANT, *shouting and clattering wood. The eagle flies away in fear and the puppet frees himself from the meat and stands by its side. The* MERCHANT *who has been shouting comes to inspect the slaughtered sheep. He doesn't see the puppet.*

MERCHANT. No diamonds? What a catastrophe! However could that have happened?

ES-SINDIBAD. Hello, friend.

MERCHANT. Who are you? What the devil are you doing here?

ES-SINDIBAD. Do not be alarmed, sir. I am an honest man, a sailor by profession. My story is extraordinary and the adventure that has brought me to these mountains is more strange and wonderful than you've ever heard before. But first, please accept some of these diamonds, which I myself gathered in the valley below.

He gives the MERCHANT *some diamonds.*

These will bring you all the riches you could wish for.

MERCHANT. A thousand thanks, good man.

ES-SINDIBAD. When the other merchants heard me talking to their friend, they trooped over.

Other MERCHANT *puppets come over.*

They greeted and congratulated me on my remarkable escape
and took me with them. I told them my story.

MERCHANT 2. God has granted you a charmed life. For no one
has set foot in the valley and come out alive.

MERCHANT 3. Heaven be praised.

ES-SINDIBAD. They gave me food and drink and I slept
soundly for many hours.

At daybreak, we set off on our journey over the great mountains together. On the way, I exchanged some of my diamonds
for rich merchandise and supplies, including a magic lantern
and a flying carpet.

We traded from port to port and island to island, till finally
we reached Baghdad, the City of Peace. When I arrived
home, ladened with diamonds and fine goods from my
travels, I gave alms to the poor and presents to my friends
and family. Then I went on to live the carefree life you see
me living now.

SHAHRAZAD. When Es-Sindibad had finished telling his story,
he gave Es-Sindibad the Porter a hundred pieces of gold.

The Porter returned many times to the house of his illustrious
friend, to hear tales of his other six voyages, and the two lived
in friendship for the rest of their lives.

Dawn

SHAHRAYAR's room. Dawn.

Sound of a sword being sharpened.

SHAHRAYAR. This sailor seems to survive every danger he
faces. Is no challenge too great for him?

SHAHRAZAD. Heaven has blessed him with the gift of
cunning, Your Majesty.

SHAHRAYAR. Does cunning come from Heaven, really? I
thought it belonged in the other place.

Enter the the VIZIER *expectantly.*

Word has reached me, Shahrazad, that the people are praising your name for saving their daughters over these last few months. You are quite a heroine. Are you proud of yourself?

SHAHRAZAD. If I please the people, then I please the King, as King and people are one.

SHAHRAYAR. I hope for the people's sake that the well of your stories does not dry up.

SHAHRAZAD. Yes, My Lord.

SHAHRAYAR. For I have given my word.

SHAHRAZAD. And a king's word is as precious as water.

SHAHRAYAR. Well, aren't you afraid?

SHAHRAZAD. I may be afraid of dying. But not of death. I have been blessed with a life filled with joy. I would rather have a short joyful life, than a long life in the darkness. Life without joy is a living death.

Pause.

SHAHRAYAR *nods to the* VIZIER.

SHAHRAYAR, DINARZAD *and the* VIZIER *catch each other's eyes.*

Exit the VIZIER.

As day turns to night they go to bed.

Listen…

How Abu Hassan Broke Wind

SHAHRAZAD. Is it said that in the city of Kaukaban in Yemen, there was a man who was the wealthiest of merchants called Abu Hassan. His wife died when she was very young and his friends were always pressing him to marry again.

ABU. So, weary of being nagged, Abu Hassan approached an old woman…

MARRIAGE BROKER. a marriage broker…

BRIDE. who found him a wife with eyes as dark as a desert night and a face as fresh as the dawn.

ABU. He arranged a sumptuous wedding banquet and invited…

UNCLE. uncles…

AUNT. and aunts…

PREACHER. preachers…

FAKIR. and fakirs…

FRIEND. friends…

FOE. and foes…

SHAHRAYAR *now joins the world of his stories as a guest.*

SHAHRAYAR. and the great…

SHAHRAZAD. and the good…

SHAHRAYAR *and* SHAHRAZAD. from all around.

ALL. The whole house was thrown open for feasting.

UNCLE *and* AUNT. There was rice of five colours…

FAKIR. sherberts of many more…

FRIEND. goats stuffed with walnuts…

FOE. and almonds and pistachios…

SHAHRAYAR *and* SHAHRAZAD. and a whole roast camel.

ALL. So they ate and drank and made merry…

BRIDE. and the bride was displayed, as is the custom, in her seven dresses to the women...

WOMEN. who couldn't take their eyes off her.

ABU. At last, the bridegroom was summoned to go up to his wife...

BRIDE. who sat on a golden throne...

ABU. and he rose with stately dignity from the sofa. When all of a sudden he let fly a huge and deafening fart.

A huge and deafening fart is heard.

AUNT. Immediately each guest turned to his neighbour...

FAKIR. and busied himself in pressing conversation...

ALL. as if his life depended on it.

ABU. But a fire of shame was lit in Abu Hassan's heart. So he excused himself and instead of going to his wife, went down to the stables, saddled his horse and rode off, weeping bitter tears through the blackness of the night.

In time he reached Lahej, where he boarded a ship bound for India and landed in Calicut on the Malabar Coast. Here he met with many fellow Arabs who introduced him to the King.

KING. And the King trusted him and made him Captain of his bodyguard.

ABU. After ten years of peace and well-being, he longed to see his homeland like a lost child longs for its mother. The homesickness grew so great that he thought he would die of it. So, without taking leave of the King, he set off. By and by he reached the hill that overlooked his home town. His eyes burned with tears when he saw his old house and he said to himself:

I hope no one recognises me. I shall wander round the outskirts and listen to the people's gossip. God grant no one remembers my shameful deed.

He trudged around for seven days and seven nights, until he found himself sitting on the doorstep of a hut. From inside, he heard the voice of a young girl...

GIRL. Mother, tell me what day I was born. One of my friends wants to tell my fortune.

MOTHER. You were born on one of the most memorable nights in the history of this country, a night so monumental that it will be enshrined in our records till the very end of time, a night so talked about that everyone in the land, from king to beggar, remembers the date. For you were born on the very same night that Abu Hassan did his historic fart.

ABU jumps up and runs away.

SHAHRAZAD. And he didn't stop travelling till he arrived back in India, where he remained for the rest of his days.

Awakening

SHAHRAYAR*'s room. Dawn.*

Sound of a sword being sharpened.

SHAHRAYAR *has turned his back to* SHAHRAZAD. *He is smiling.*

SHAHRAZAD. Did you enjoy the story, My Lord?

SHAHRAYAR *giggles, laughs, then a huge, belly-aching laugh rips out of him.* DINARZAD *and* SHAHRAZAD *start laughing too.*

Enter the VIZIER.

He stares at SHAHRAYAR, *shocked.*

Lights fade to a solo spot on the laughing King.

Blackout.

End of Act One.

ACT TWO

The Story of the Wife Who Wouldn't Eat

SIDI 1 *tells this story to* HAROUN, *and* SIDI 2 *acts it out in flashback. They are identifiable as the same person by distinctive items of the same clothing.*

SHAHRAZAD. The great Caliph Haroun Al-Rashid often went out into the city of Baghdad in disguise, to find out more about the lives of his people. Once on such a trip, he saw a huge crowd of spectators in the market square.

Enter AMINA *as a horse and* SIDI 1, *who rides her around the stage furiously.*

They were watching a handsome young man ride a horse at full speed. He was whipping her so harshly that she was wrapped in ribbons of blood.

HAROUN. The Caliph was shocked by the young man's cruelty, and he asked his loyal Vizier to summon the young man to the Palace. The following day, he came and kissed the ground before Haroun Al-Rashid. The Caliph asked his name and he replied:

SIDI 1. Sidi Nu'uman.

HAROUN. I have seen horses trained all my life, Sidi Nu'uman, but never, I am glad to say, in such a cruel, heartless way as you did yesterday. The spectators were horrified and so was I. In front of me now, you do not seem such a fearsome man, yet I am told, you do the same brutal thing every day. I would like to know the cause and have called you here, this morning, to give me a full and thorough explanation.

SIDI 1. I dare say that the way I treat my horse may seem cruel and heartless. When you hear the reasons why, you will see that I am more worthy of pity than blame.

HAROUN. Tell me your story...

SIDI 1. As is our country's custom, I married having never seen or met my wife. When she took off her veil after our wedding,

I was pleased. I had feared she might be old, ugly and wrinkled, but she seemed charming.

We see SIDI 2 *unveil* AMINA. *She lays out two plates of rice.*

The day after our wedding, I sat down to lunch and began to eat my rice, as usual – heartily, with a spoon.

As he speaks we see this.

My wife, however, pushed her spoon aside...

AMINA *pulls a little case out of her pocket. She opens it and takes out a small pair of tweezers. She uses these to pick up the rice and nibble at it, grain by grain.*

SIDI 2 *watches her, agog. She eats politely, as if this was the proper thing to do.*

Surprised at this, I said to her...

SIDI 2. Amina.

SIDI 1. For that was her name...

SIDI 2. Is it a family custom of yours to eat your rice so daintily or do you have a small appetite?

AMINA *carries on eating with the tweezers.*

If you are doing it to save money, then don't worry, I promise we could afford ten thousand plates of rice and still have money to spare. Don't hold back, my dear Amina, but enjoy your food as I do.

SIDI 1. My politeness and patience fell on deaf ears.

She continues to eat slowly, grain by grain.

The following night, at supper, she did exactly the same thing. And the next night and the next.

I knew it was impossible for anyone to live on so little food. So, I decided to get to the bottom of this mystery.

One night when Amina thought me fast asleep...

SIDI 2 *acts out the following.*

she slithered softly out of bed. I pretended to keep my eyes shut, but secretly was watching her like a hungry hawk.

AMINA *dresses and tiptoes out of the room.*

The moment she turned her back, I got up and put on my robe. I ran down to the front door and followed her by the eerie light of the moon, to a nearby graveyard. I hid behind a wall and peeked over, and I saw Amina with a ghoul.

AMINA *dances a monstrous dance with the* GHOUL.

I watched with horror as they dug up a body that had been buried that day, cut the flesh into several pieces and ate it up, slavering and slobbering over their sickening feast in a way that makes me shudder to think about.

As they were filling up the grave with earth, I hurried home, taking care to leave the door as I found it.

SIDI 2 *goes to bed. As* AMINA *approaches, he feigns sleep. She gets into bed beside him.*

AMINA *belches.*

The next day, at dinner, she started to eat in her usual way.

They eat together as before, AMINA *again eats with tweezers.*

SIDI 2. Amina, won't you eat some more?

AMINA *shakes her head.*

Are you sure?

AMINA *nods.*

You remember, Amina, how surprised I was when I first saw you eat your food in such a strange and sparing fashion. I'm sure you also recall how frequently I urged you to taste the many foods I had flavoured and prepared innumerable different ways to please you. It seems that none of my efforts have paid off, for still you pick at your food in the same curious way. I have never lost my temper, and would be sorry now to make you feel uneasy, but I should like to ask you a question, my dear wife. Does the food at my table not taste better than dead flesh?

SIDI 1. It was then that I discovered that Amina was an evil sorceress.

AMINA *dips her hand into a basin of water and throws it into*
SIDI 2*'s face, with the words:*

AMINA.

By the power of water drawn from a bog,
Nosy wretch, turn into a dog!

SIDI 2 *becomes a dog and yaps pathetically at* AMINA. *She*
grabs a stick and chases him with it, beating him. He outruns
her. She grabs his tail, meanly. He whimpers and nips her. He
runs off, barking and howling.

SIDI 1. I ran out of the house and into the street. Before long, all
the local stray dogs were chasing after me.

Chase sequence. Whole COMPANY *as dogs chasing* SIDI
NU'UMAN *through the audience and biting him where*
possible.

I took refuge in the doorway of a Baker who was cheerful and
kind.

BAKER. Hello, dog.

The BAKER *throws* SIDI 2 *a piece of bread. He licks the*
BAKER*'s face and wags his tail to show appreciation. The*
BAKER *laughs.* SIDI 2 *then eats the piece of bread.*

SIDI 1. The Baker let me stay in the shop and gave me a place to
sleep.

If I was out of sight, he would call...

BAKER. Chance!

SIDI 1. which was the name he gave me.

BAKER. Chance!!

SIDI 2 *comes scooting in and jumps and flies up to his master,*
running round and round, being a playful, obedient dog.

SIDI 1. One day, a woman came into the shop to buy some
bread. She paid with several coins, one of which was false,
and completely worthless. My master noticed the bad coin
and gave it back, asking for another.

CUSTOMER 1. There is nothing wrong with this coin.

BAKER. Come off it.

CUSTOMER 1. The coin is good.

BAKER. Lady, this coin is so obviously fake even my dog could pick it out.

CUSTOMER 1. Go on then. Ask him.

BAKER. Very well. Chance! Chance!

SIDI 2 approaches.

Look at these coins, Chance. Tell me which one is false.

SIDI 2 examines and sniffs each coin and then sets his paw on the bad one, separates it from the rest, and stares his master in the face, to await approval.

SIDI 1. The Baker was staggered. The woman changed her bad coin for a good one and left, stunned into silence. She was sure to tell everyone she met about me. Before long, word spread throughout the city about the friendly Baker with the miraculous dog with the magic gift of telling good money from bad. People came from far and wide to see me show my skill, and everyone who did, bought a loaf of bread. Soon, my master had more business than he could manage and he became a wealthy man.

One day, another woman came to buy some bread.

CUSTOMER 2 throws down six coins on the counter. SIDI 2 places his paw on one of the coins and looks up at the woman.

CUSTOMER 2. Yes, you are quite right – that is the bad coin.

She beckons for SIDI 2 to come with her. He hesitates for a moment and then follows her out of the shop.

SIDI 1. Several streets away, she stopped at a house and beckoned me in.

CUSTOMER 2. You won't regret following me.

He follows her in.

SIDI 1. When I went in I saw a beautiful young lady with a smile as sweet as hope.

CUSTOMER 2. Daughter, I have brought you the famous
   Baker's dog. Remember when I first heard about him, I had a
   hunch he was a man changed into a dog. Now, tell me,
   daughter, am I mistaken in my suspicion?

SORCERESS. No, Mother, you are not. As I shall prove.

   SORCERESS *dips her hand into a basin of water and throws
   it into* SIDI 2*'s face, with the words:*

      If you were dogged by evil plan,
      By the power of water change back to a man!

   SIDI 2 *changes back into a man. He throws himself at the*
   SORCERESS*'s feet.*

SIDI 2. Thank you, thank you, thank you. My debt to you is
   greater than I could ever repay.

SIDI 1. After I had told her who I was, I gave an account of my
   marriage to Amina, her curious eating, the horrible sight I saw
   in the graveyard, my attempt to reason with her and how I
   came to be changed into a dog.

SORCERESS. I know Amina of old. She must be punished once
   and for all. Take this bottle. Go home immediately and hide in
   your bedroom. As soon as Amina comes in, throw this potion
   at her, pronouncing clearly and boldly:

      By the power of potion brewed over time,
      Receive the punishment for your crime!

SIDI 2.
      By the power of potion brewed over time…

SIDI 2 *and* SORCERESS.
      Receive the punishment for your crime!

SORCERESS. I will tell you no more. You shall see the result.

   SORCERESS *and* CUSTOMER 2 *gently laugh.* SIDI 2 *waits
   in his bedroom.*

   AMINA *enters and meets* SIDI 2 *face to face. She screams
   and turns, about to run to the door. He throws the potion over
   her. She freezes.*

SIDI 2.

> By the power of potion brewed over time,
> Receive the punishment for your...
> Receive the punishment for your...
> Receive the punishment for your...

He looks for help from the audience.

AUDIENCE. Crime!

SIDI 2. Rhyme? (*Etc.*)

AUDIENCE. Crime!

SIDI 2.

> By the power of potion brewed over time,
> Receive the punishment for your crime!

AMINA transforms into a horse. SIDI 2 grabs her by the mane. He then rides her in a repeat of the first time we met SIDI 1. SIDI 2 echoes the first entrance of SIDI 1 riding and beating his horse.

SIDI 1. And I have beaten and reproached her the same way every day, ever since. I hope Your Majesty will now agree that I have shown such a cruel and wicked woman more patience than she deserves.

HAROUN. Your story is well told. If true, then the wickedness of your wife is inexcusable. If false, your invention deserves praise, for eloquence is lawful magic. Therefore I can forgive some of your harshness towards your horse. However, being changed into an animal is surely punishment enough and you must not hurt her any more. Bitterness is like a deadly, climbing weed. If it lays its roots in your thoughts, it will not stop until it has strangled your heart and poisoned your soul. To be free, you must forgive.

SHAHRAYAR has approached and watches HAROUN and then SIDI closely.

SHAHRAZAD. The wise Caliph signified by the bowing of his head that Sidi Nu'uman was free to go. Sidi Nu'uman kissed the ground before him and retired.

SIDI strokes the horse and leads it away.

Promise

SHAHRAYAR*'s room. Dawn.*

Sound of a sword being sharpened.

Enter the VIZIER. *He is now an old, old man.*

He has just entered when SHAHRAYAR *signals for him to go. Without stopping he turns round and exits.*

SHAHRAZAD. The day melted into night.

DINARZAD. And an hour before daybreak...

SHAHRAYAR. King Shahrayar said:

What story do you have for me tonight?

SHAHRAZAD. A trifling tale, My Lord.

SHAHRAYAR. One of many hundreds of trifling tales you have told me already.

SHAHRAZAD. Eight hundred and seventeen, My Lord.

SHAHRAYAR. Your wily woman's tongue has saved your pretty head eight hundred and seventeen times. That's a long time.

DINARZAD. Two years, two months, three weeks and four days.

SHAHRAYAR. I can't seem to resist your stories, my crafty Queen. Your trick is working. Well, go on. Begin.

SHAHRAZAD *doesn't speak.*

Speak.

SHAHRAZAD *remains silent.*

I'm listening.

She is still silent.

I command you to tell me your story.

SHAHRAZAD *whispers to* DINARZAD.

SHAHRAYAR. Well, what is she saying?

DINARZAD. She says she dare not speak. In case she tries to trick you with her cunning woman's words.

SHAHRAYAR. Tell her I want to hear the story.

DINARZAD *whispers to* SHAHRAZAD. SHAHRAZAD *whispers back.*

DINARZAD. She says, 'Are you sure?'

SHAHRAYAR. Tell her 'Yes'!

DINARZAD *whispers to her again.* SHAHRAZAD *whispers back.*

DINARZAD. 'Really sure?'

SHAHRAYAR. Yes.

DINARZAD *goes to whisper to her.*

ONE MORE WHISPER AND I'LL HAVE BOTH YOUR HEADS OFF!

SHAHRAZAD. Your Majesty.

SHAHRAYAR. Wife.

SHAHRAZAD. What would you do if the well of my stories runs dry?

SHAHRAYAR. But that will never happen. (*Beat.*) Will it?

SHAHRAZAD. As there are so many grains of sand in the desert, there are only so many stories in my head. They are sure to run out one day. And on that day, I must die. For you have given your word.

SHAHRAYAR. I have.

SHAHRAZAD. And a king's word is as precious as water.

SHAHRAYAR. It is.

SHAHRAZAD. Shall I start then?

SHAHRAYAR. What?

SHAHRAZAD. My story.

SHAHRAYAR. Of course.

SHAHRAZAD. Very well.

Listen…

The Story of the Envious Sisters

SHAHRAZAD. There was once a King in Persia called Khusrau
Shah. One evening, he was walking with his Vizier in a poor
area of the city when he overheard laughter coming from the
humblest house in the street. He approached, and peeking
through a crack in the door, he saw three sisters sitting on a
sofa having an after-dinner chat. They were talking about
wishes.

ELDEST SISTER. I wish I could marry the King's baker. For
then I would eat my belly full of bread. And Royal bread is
the finest in the city.

SECOND SISTER. I wish I could marry the King's cook. For
then I would enjoy the most excellent meats. And meats are
much tastier than bread.

YOUNGEST SISTER. I wish I could marry the King. For I
would give him a beautiful baby Prince, with hair like threads
of silver and gold. When he cried his tears would be pearls
and when he smiled his crimson lips would be fresh rosebuds.

KING. The next day at the Palace, the King ordered his Vizier to
bring the three sisters before him.

They kiss the floor before him.

They stand.

Last night you each made a wish. You wished to marry my
baker. Your wish shall be granted today. You wished to marry
my cook. Your wish shall be granted today. And you wished
to marry me. Your wish shall be granted today.

The YOUNGEST *throws herself on floor.*

YOUNGEST. Forgive me, Your Majesty, but my wish was only
made by way of fun. I am not worthy of this honour. I pray
you, pardon me my boldness.

The two ELDER SISTERS *reluctantly copy.*

ELDER SISTERS. Forgive us, Your Majesty... .

KING (*interrupting*). Silence! It shall be so. What I command is law.

THREE SISTERS. The weddings were celebrated that day...

ELDER SISTERS. but in very different style.

ELDEST. The eldest sister's wedding was celebrated in the pantry surrounded by sacks of flour.

SECOND. The second sister's wedding was celebrated in the kitchen surrounded by pots and pans.

YOUNGEST. The youngest sister's wedding was celebrated in the Royal Garden surrounded by jasmine and almond blossom.

ELDEST. Although their wishes had been granted...

SECOND. the two elder sisters felt the difference between their weddings and their sister's...

ELDER SISTERS. grossly unfair.

ELDEST. Their hearts were seized by a snake-like envy...

SECOND. which not only strangled their own joy...

YOUNGEST. but pierced their younger sister's happiness like a spiteful fang.

ELDEST. Well, Sister, what do you think of our grand little sister? I'm not being nasty, but isn't she a fine one to be Queen?

SECOND. The King must be bewitched, to be so taken with the little madam. You are much more deserving. In fairness, he should have chosen you.

ELDEST. I wouldn't have batted an eyelid if the King had picked you. But that he should prefer that pert little slut makes my blood boil.

SECOND. Who's she to be wearing a crown? I'll be damned if I'm going to bow and scrape to her.

ELDEST. Setting herself above us like that. Thinking she's the best.

SECOND. Looking down her nose.

ELDEST. Well, I won't stand for it.

SECOND. Me neither.

ELDEST. It's time for action.

SECOND. I quite agree. We'll knock her down a peg or two.

ELDEST. From then on, whenever they visited the Queen, their sister...

SECOND. they would keep their vipers' tongues hidden behind the painted smiles.

YOUNGEST. And she would welcome them warmly and simply and treat them with the same love she always had.

Some months after their marriage, the Queen found she was expecting a baby.

ELDEST. The sisters came to give their best wishes...

SECOND. and offered to be by their sister's side when the baby was born...

ELDER SISTERS. as her midwives.

YOUNGEST. The Queen gave birth to a young Prince as bright as morning.

The actor playing BAHMAN *makes the sound of a baby crying.*

ELDEST. But neither his sweetness...

SECOND. nor his beauty...

ELDER SISTERS. could melt the icy hearts of the ruthless sisters.

ELDEST. They wrapped him carelessly in a blanket, dropped him in a basket and floated him down a stream which ran past the Queen's apartment.

SECOND. They then declared:

ELDER SISTERS. She gave birth to a dead dog.

They produce the dead dog.

KING. When the King was told, the world turned dark before his eyes and he ordered the Queen's head to be cut off.

KING'S VIZIER. But the kind Vizier stopped him, pleading that the Queen could not be blamed for something that was not of her doing, but nature's.

BAHMAN. Meanwhile, the basket in which the little baby lay floated downstream past the Palace and through the King's Gardens.

STEWARD. By happy chance, the Steward of the King's Garden was walking past. When he saw the basket bobbing by, he fished it out and peered in. He was astonished to find, fast asleep, a tiny baby.

The Steward took the baby to his house and showed him to his wife.

STEWARD'S WIFE. His wife had never had children of her own. She received the child with great joy, and took pleasure in looking after him as if he was hers.

YOUNGEST. A year later, the Queen gave birth to another baby Prince.

The actor playing PERVIZ *makes the sound of a baby crying.*

ELDER SISTERS. The envious sisters were no kinder to him than the first.

ELDEST. They dropped him in a basket and floated him down the stream...

SECOND. announcing:

ELDER SISTERS. She gave birth to a dead cat.

They show the dead cat.

KING. This time the King was determined to cut off the young Queen's head...

KING'S VIZIER. but again the Vizier stopped him, pleading:

Let her live.

STEWARD. By happy chance, the Steward was walking by the stream again that day when he saw the second basket bobbing by. He took this child to his wife and asked her to take as good care of it as the first.

STEWARDS'S WIFE. This suited her as well as it did her husband.

QUEEN. The third time the Queen became pregnant, she gave birth to a Princess.

The actor playing PARIZADE *makes the sound of a baby crying.*

ELDER SISTERS. The poor child suffered the same fate as her brothers.

SECOND. This time the sisters couldn't find an animal.

ELDEST. So they took a piece of wood and showed it, saying:

ELDER SISTERS. She gave birth to a mole.

KING. The King could no longer contain himself.

This woman wants to fill my Palace with monsters. She is a monster herself and I will rid the world of her.

KING'S VIZIER. Your Majesty, give me leave to speak.

KING. You have spoken too much already.

VIZIER. I beg you, My Lord, hear me.

The KING'S VIZIER *prostrates himself. The* KING *is surprised and embarrassed by this.*

KING. Stand up, man.

The KING'S VIZIER *does so. The* KING *gestures for him to speak.*

VIZIER. Your Majesty, laws are made to punish crimes. The three strange births of the Queen are not crimes, for she did nothing to bring them about. Every day around the world there are thousands of women who give birth to babies that are sick or deformed, some are dead. Such women are to be pitied, not punished. Show remorse, My Lord, take the higher path, and let her live.

KING. Very well, Vizier, I will give her her life. But it shall be on this condition: that every day, for the rest of her life, she wishes she were dead. Let a cell be built next to the Great Mosque, with iron bars for windows, and throw her in. Dress her in clothes that scratch her skin. And everyone that goes past shall spit in her face. Vizier, see it done. Now.

KING'S VIZIER. The Vizier knew better than to question the King in his rage. So he did as he was told...

ELDER SISTERS. to the great pleasure of the two envious sisters.

The YOUNGEST *is thrown into a cell.* PASSERS-BY *spit.*

STEWARD. That same day, the Steward was walking past the stream, and he took the third child to his wife and asked her to mind her, as well as the first two...

STEWARD'S WIFE. which she did most gladly.

BAHMAN *and* PERVIZ. The two Princes...

PARIZADE. and the Princess...

STEWARD. were brought up by the Steward...

STEWARD'S WIFE. and his wife...

STEWARD *and* STEWARD'S WIFE. with all the tenderness of a true father and mother.

BAHMAN, PERVIZ *and* PARIZADE. They were named after ancient kings and queens of Persia.

BAHMAN. The eldest Prince was named Bahman. He was gentle and kind.

PERVIZ. The second was named Perviz. He was bold and head-strong.

PARIZADE. And the Princess was named Parizade.

BAHMAN. She was enchantingly beautiful...

PERVIZ. and exceptionally clever.

STEWARD. As soon as the Princes were old enough, the Steward provided them with the best teachers money could buy.

PARIZADE. Even though the Princess was much younger, she would join in all their lessons and would often outshine them.

STEWARD. The Steward was so delighted with his adopted children that he set about building them a grand country house. He decked the rooms with priceless paintings and splendid furniture. He filled the garden with blazing flowers and fragrant shrubs. Then he stocked the nearby land with deer, so that the Princes and Princess could go hunting.

He lived in the house with the two Princes, Bahman and Perviz, and Princess Parizade for six months, when one day he shut his eyes and died.

BAHMAN. His wife had died some years before…

PERVIZ. and his death was so sudden that he never had a chance to tell them the secret of their birth.

PARIZADE. The Princes and Princess wept bitter tears of grief for the man they thought their father.

BAHMAN, PERVIZ *and* PARIZADE. But they were comforted by their beautiful house, and lived there together in harmony.

WOMAN. One day, when the two Princes were out hunting, an old religious woman arrived at the house. When she had said her prayers, she sat down with Parizade and chatted with her.

PARIZADE. Eventually, Parizade asked her what she thought of the house?

WOMAN. Madam, it would be the king of houses but for three things.

PARIZADE. And what three things are they? I will do what I can to secure them.

WOMAN. The first of these things is the Talking Bird. This will draw a thousand coloured birds around it. The second is the Singing Tree. This will play a haunting harmony. The third is the Golden Water. This will form an everlasting fountain.

PARIZADE. I've never heard of such curious, wonderful things. Would you kindly tell me where they are?

WOMAN. Towards India, on the road that lies before your house. Whoever you send must travel twenty days. On the twentieth day they must ask the first person they meet where the Talking Bird, Singing Tree and Golden Water are. They shall be told.

If you find these three things, child, they will lead you to the truth about yourself.

PARIZADE. What do you mean?

WOMAN. And a fine lady shall be freed.

PARIZADE. I don't understand.

WOMAN. The road that lies before your house.

Exit WOMAN.

PARIZADE. 'Towards India, on the road that lies before your house. Twenty days along.'

BAHMAN. When her brothers returned...

PERVIZ. they found their sister with her head weighed down...

BAHMAN *and* PERVIZ. as if her thoughts were made of lead.

BAHMAN. What's the matter, Sister?

PARIZADE. Nothing.

PERVIZ. Has someone offended you? If anybody's offended you, I will revenge it.

PARIZADE. No one's offended me.

BAHMAN. Well, what's wrong?

Pause.

PERVIZ. What are you hiding from us?

BAHMAN. We're your brothers, remember? We share every-thing. Don't shut us out.

PARIZADE. Very well, I'll tell you, but you'll think I'm mad.

BAHMAN. We would never think that. Would we, Perviz?

PERVIZ. Well, there was that time...

BAHMAN (*interrupting*). Perviz!

PERVIZ. We'd never think you're mad.

PARIZADE. Parizade told her brothers all that the old woman had said.

BAHMAN. Tell me the way there and I will leave tomorrow.

PARIZADE. No, Brother, the risks on the open road are too great. There are bandits, wild animals. You could be killed.

PERVIZ. Why don't I go instead? You're the head of the house-hold, Brother. It doesn't make sense for you to be away from home for such a long time. You have so many duties to attend to, with the staff and the grounds. It's more practical for me to go. I'm not afraid.

BAHMAN. I have made a promise and I will honour it. Brother, I will leave you in charge of the house.

PERVIZ. Very well.

BAHMAN. Early the next morning, Prince Bahman prepared his horse.

PARIZADE *and* BAHMAN *embrace*.

BAHMAN *takes out a knife*.

Here, Sister, take this knife, and every now and then, look at the blade. If it is clean, it is a sign I am alive.

If it is stained with blood, then you must believe me dead, and pray for me.

On the twentieth day of his journey, he saw, by the side of the road, a Dervish, sitting under a tree.

BAHMAN. Good day, good Father, may Heaven grant you a long life. I have come from far in search of the Talking Bird, the Singing Tree and the Golden Water. Could you show me the way to them?

DERVISH. Friendship forbids me to tell you.

BAHMAN. Why?

DERVISH. A great number of fine gentlemen, as brave and courageous as you, have passed by here and asked me the very same question. Against my better judgement, I have told them the way and not one of them has ever come back. Son, if the gift of life means anything to you, go home now.

BAHMAN. I have a knife. If anyone attacks me, I shall use it.

DERVISH. What if your enemies are invisible?

BAHMAN. Good Father, know this: I have ridden through heat, rain and snow, across mountains, deserts and rivers. In twenty days I have barely slept or eaten, been alone day and night, and faced countless threats. I've never given up and I'm never going to give up because I've made a promise. I would sooner die than break it. No matter what you say, no matter how many times you warn me, you will never persuade me to alter my course.

DERVISH. Take this ball.

A ball appears.

When you are on horseback, place it before you. It will start rolling. Follow it to the foot of a mountain where it will stop. Leave your horse and start climbing the slope. You will see a large number of black stones and hear many threatening voices urging you to turn around. They will try everything they can to stop you reaching the top of the mountain. But remember, whatever you hear behind you, no matter how cruel, vicious or threatening: do not look back. For if you do, you will be turned into black stone like the other gentlemen before you. If you manage to escape this danger and reach the top of the mountain, you will see a cage. In that cage is the Bird you seek. Ask him for the Singing Tree and Golden Water and he will show you.

BAHMAN. Thank you, good Father.

DERVISH. May the Heavens preserve you.

BAHMAN. Bahman mounted his horse and placed the ball before him.

The ball rolls away. BAHMAN *follows it. When it reaches the foot of the mountain, it stops.*

The COMPANY *become stones.*

He looked up the mountain and saw the black stones, but had not gone three steps when the voices started:

Their voices start quietly and escalate with every step he takes, until they reach a murderous and deafening cacophony. Each actor repeats/improvises around the lines below. The same format is used for each attempt.

ACTOR 1. You'll never make it up to the top. A little weakling like you?

Laughter, etc.

ACTOR 2. Turn around. There's a wolf behind you.

ACTOR 3. That's it. Carry on. Just see what awaits you at the top of the slope! You are walking towards your death. (*Etc.*)

ACTOR 4. Go home. Your family are ill. They need your help. (*Etc.*)

ACTOR 5. You snivelling little wretch. You cockroach. You snake. (*Etc.*)

ACTOR 6. I've got a surprise for you, sweet child, come and get your surprise.

ACTOR 7. It's the devil's trick. Turn back. This is the voice of your father. Turn back.

Eventually, BAHMAN'*s courage gives way and he turns. Instantly he is turned to stone.*

PARIZADE. Just then, Princess Parizade pulled the knife out of its sheath, as she did many times a day, to see if her brother was safe. Her heart froze to stone in her chest when she saw that the point was dripping with blood.

She throws it down.

Oh, my dear brother, I have been the cause of your death. Why did I listen to the old religious woman? Why did she tell me of the Bird, the Tree and the Water? I wish I'd never met her.

PERVIZ. Our dear brother's death must not prevent us from pursuing our plan. Tomorrow I shall go myself.

PARIZADE. The Princess begged him not to go...

PERVIZ. but he was determined.

> Before he went, he left her a necklace of a hundred pearls, telling her, from time to time, to run her fingers along them.

> If they move, I am alive. If they are fixed, then you know I am dead.

PERVIZ. On the twentieth day of his journey, Prince Perviz met the Dervish. Prince Perviz asked him, the same way his brother had, where he could find the Talking Bird, Singing Tree and Golden Water...

DERVISH. And the Dervish pleaded with Prince Perviz to go home, as he had to Prince Bahman.

PERVIZ. Good Father, I have thought too long and hard about this plan to give up now.

DERVISH. As Prince Perviz could not be stopped, the Dervish handed him a ball, and told him to follow it to the foot of the mountain. Then he gave Prince Perviz the same warning he had given to Prince Bahman, about the black stones and the threatening voices.

> But remember, whatever you hear behind you, however cruel, vicious or threatening: do not look back.

PERVIZ. Prince Perviz took leave of the Dervish with a low bow and placed the ball before him.

The ball rolls away. When it reaches the foot of the mountain, it stops.

Full COMPANY *become stones, as before. Same escalation of voices, but louder.*

PERVIZ *gets very near the* BIRD *when the other voices stop and a male voice just behind him says:*

STONE. Stop, foolish youth. I shall punish your insolence with my sword.

When he hears this, PERVIZ *draws his sword and turns around. He is immediately turned to stone.*

PARIZADE. Just then, Princess Parizade was pulling on the pearls of her necklace, as she did many times a day, when all of a sudden they stuck to the string. She knew then for certain that Prince Perviz was dead.

The next morning, she set out on the same road as her brothers. On the twentieth day, she met the Dervish.

PARIZADE. Parizade asked the Dervish where she could find the Talking Bird, Singing Tree and Golden Water.

DERVISH. And the Dervish pleaded with her to turn round, as he had with her brothers.

PARIZADE. And give up my plan? I am sure I shall succeed.

DERVISH. Because she would not heed his advice, the Dervish gave her the ball and repeated the warning he had given to Prince Bahman and Prince Perviz about the dreadful danger of the black stones and the threatening voices.

PARIZADE. From what you say, the only danger I face is getting to the cage without hearing the threatening voices. But that can be overcome quite simply.

DERVISH. How?

PARIZADE. By stopping my ears with cotton.

DERVISH. Of all the people who have asked me the way, I cannot think of any who have thought of that. If you must go, by all means try your trick. But remember, if you should hear anything on the mountain, however cruel, vicious or threatening: do not look back.

PARIZADE. After thanking him, she rode away and placed the ball before her.

The ball rolls away. When it reaches the foot of the mountain it stops. She puts cotton in her ears.

Full COMPANY become stones as before. Same escalation of volume, but even louder. She gets close to the BIRD, who is a glove puppet in a cage operated by the YOUNGEST SISTER.

BIRD. Brave lady, if I have to be a slave I would rather be your slave than any in the world, since you have won me so courageously. From this moment, I swear a lifelong loyalty to you and promise to fulfil your every need.

PARIZADE. Thank you, Bird.

BIRD. I know who you really are and I can tell you: you are not who you think you are.

PARIZADE. What do you mean?

BIRD. You will find out in God's good time.

PARIZADE. Bird, I have been told there is a Singing Tree nearby. I want to know where it is.

BIRD. Turn around and you will see a wood behind you. You will find the Tree there.

She picks up the BIRD.

PARIZADE. The Princess went into the wood. Her ears soon lead her to the Singing Tree.

COMPANY *become the Singing Tree*.

BIRD. Break off a branch and plant it in your garden. In a short time, it will grow into as fine a Tree as you see here.

PARIZADE. Bird, I also want to find the Golden Water. Can you show me to it?

COMPANY *become a fountain*.

The Bird showed her the place that was nearby and she went and filled a silver flask she had brought.

I have one more request. My brothers were turned into black stones. I want you to free them.

BIRD. I have already done quite enough for today. I'm tired.

PARIZADE. I thought you said you were my slave and you would fulfil my every need?

BIRD. Yes, I did, didn't I? I can't get used to this slave business. It doesn't sit right with me.

PARIZADE. Please, Bird.

BIRD. Oh, very well then, since you asked me nicely. Look around and you will see a pitcher of water.

PARIZADE. I see it.

BIRD. Pick it up, go down the hill and sprinkle some on every black stone. You shall soon find your brothers.

PARIZADE picks up the pitcher and goes down the hill, sprinkling water on every black stone. As soon as she does so, it immediately turns into a man or a horse and they run away.

She finds her brothers.

PERVIZ. Sister!

BAHMAN (*to* PERVIZ). Brother!

PARIZADE (*to* BAHMAN). Brother!

PERVIZ. Sister!

They embrace.

They notice the BIRD.

BAHMAN. You did it!

PERVIZ. You did it!

BAHMAN *and* PERVIZ. She did it!

PARIZADE. I did it.

They embrace again.

PERVIZ. You saved my life!

PARIZADE. I saved your life!

BAHMAN. You saved my life!

BAHMAN *and* PERVIZ. She saved our lives.

BAHMAN and PERVIZ *prostrate themselves at* PARIZADE's *feet.*

BAHMAN. Thank you!

PERVIZ. Tha –

BIRD (*coughing*). Ahem!

PARIZADE. Forgive me, Bird. I've been rude. Bird, this is my eldest brother, Bahman.

BIRD. Charmed.

PARIZADE. And my elder brother, Perviz.

BIRD. Delighted.

PARIZADE (*to* BAHMAN). Brother, here is a branch of the Singing Tree for you to carry.

She hands it to him.

(*To* PERVIZ.) And for you, the Golden Water.

She gives this to PERVIZ.

Now, let's go home!

When the Princess arrived, she placed the cage in the garden.

As soon as the BIRD *starts to sing, other colourful birds swoop and glide around it.*

BAHMAN. Then she planted the branch of the Singing Tree.

The Tree sprouts up, each leaf singing a delightful tune and all joining together to play a harmonious concert.

PERVIZ. After that she poured the flask of Golden Water into a marble pool.

A fountain shoots up.

BAHMAN. Some days later, Prince Bahman…

PERVIZ. and Prince Perviz…

BAHMAN *and* PERVIZ. went hunting in a nearby forest.

KING. As it happened, hunting in the same forest was the King.

They bump into the KING. *They kiss the ground before him. They look up.*

Have I met you before? Who are you?

BAHMAN. Sir, we are the sons of the late Steward of your Garden.

KING. I thought I recognised you. He was a good man. A fine man. Do you live nearby?

BAHMAN. We do, My Lord.

KING. Very good. I need somewhere to rest this evening. I should like to visit you.

PERVIZ. Your Majesty, we would be honoured.

BAHMAN. Princes Bahman...

PERVIZ. and Perviz...

BAHMAN. pointed the King's courtiers in the direction of the house...

BAHMAN *and* PERVIZ. and hurried home to tell their sister.

PARIZADE. We must prepare a banquet for His Majesty.

She goes to the BIRD.

Bird, the King will be coming to visit tonight. What shall we give him to eat?

BIRD. Let your cooks prepare a dish of cucumbers stuffed with pearls.

PARIZADE. Cucumbers stuffed with pearls? Pearls are not to be eaten. That sounds revolting. Besides, where would I get enough pearls for such a dish?

BIRD. Mistress, have faith. Go now to the foot of the Singing Tree, dig under it and you will find what you want.

PARIZADE *digs and finds a precious gold box filled with pearls.*

PARIZADE. Parizade called the Head Cook to her.

Tonight you must prepare a dish of cucumbers stuffed with pearls.

HEAD COOK. Pearls? Did I hear you correctly, madam? Did you say, 'cucumbers stuffed with pearls'?

PARIZADE. I did.

PARIZADE *presents the open pearl box to the* HEAD COOK.

HEAD COOK. Madam, I am a trained culinary artiste. A cook. I prepare food. That is, things that are edible. That can be eaten. Or at the very least, licked! I am not a jeweller or a maker of decorative trinkets. I am therefore ill-equipped to make any-thing involving semi-precious stones.

PARIZADE. But cucumbers stuffed with pearls is the King's favourite dish, Cook. I'm surprised you didn't know that.

HEAD COOK. I didn't know it and if I had've been told I wouldn't have already started preparing an enormous pie stuffed with three lambs, twenty chickens, fifteen wildfowl and a chaffinch. But, what His Majesty desires, His Majesty shall receive.

PARIZADE. Thank you, Cook.

The HEAD COOK *takes the box.*

HEAD COOK. Good day to you, madam.

PARIZADE. Then, the Princess instructed the servants to make the final preparations for the visit of the King.

The KING *and the* KING'S VIZIER *arrive.* BAHMAN *and* PERVIZ *go before the* KING *and kiss the floor.*

BAHMAN *and* PERVIZ. This is our sister.

PARIZADE *kisses the floor before the* KING. *The* KING *helps her up.*

KING. Charming. She has something of her father's nobility, don't you agree, Vizier?

KING'S VIZIER. I do.

KING. The dear Steward. Such a fine man.

KING'S VIZIER. Very fine.

KING. I look forward to getting to know you, madam, after you have shown me the house.

PARIZADE. So the Princess led him to the Golden Water, Singing Tree, and Talking Bird, who sat on his perch in the hall.

BIRD. The King is welcome here. Heaven spare him and grant him a long life.

KING. Bird, I thank you and am overjoyed to have found in you the King of Birds.

The BIRD *bows.*

They sit down to eat. The HEAD COOK *arrives and ceremoniously presents the cucumbers stuffed with pearls.*

HEAD COOK. Cucumbers stuffed with pearls!

KING. Cucumbers stuffed with pearls? Pearls are not to be eaten! What is the meaning of this?

BIRD. Can Your Majesty be so amazed at seeing cucumbers stuffed with pearls? Yet you readily believe that the Queen, your wife, gave birth to a dog, a cat and a piece of wood.

KING. I believed it because I was told so by her midwives.

BIRD. Those midwives were the Queen's wicked sisters, who, out of envy and revenge, lied to Your Majesty. Awake from your sleep of ignorance: the brothers and sister you see before you are your own children. Found by the Steward of your Garden, who brought them up and educated them as his own.

KING. My heart whispered the truth from the moment I met you...

The KING *embraces his children.*

Bahman, Perviz and Parizade: Royal by name, Royal by nature.

KING, BAHMAN, PERVIZ *and* PARIZADE. By torchlight, they set out for the city on their horses.

KING. As soon as they reached the Palace, the King ordered the Vizier to bring the Queen's envious sisters immediately to trial.

KING'S VIZIER. And after they were found guilty...

The ELDER SISTERS *hold dolls of themselves up.*

SECOND. they were each cut into four pieces...

They tear the dolls up.

ELDEST. and fed to the dogs.

They 'eat' the dolls.

KING. In the meantime, the King, Khosrou Shah…

BAHMAN, PERVIZ *and* PARIZADE. followed by his three children…

BIRD. and the Talking Bird…

KING, BAHMAN, PERVIZ *and* PARIZADE. went to the Great Mosque.

The QUEEN *is freed from her cell.*

KING. I am your humble servant. I come to return what is rightfully yours. Your freedom, your crown, our children.

The KING *prostrates himself at her feet. The* QUEEN *touches his head. He kneels. The* QUEEN *reaches out to her children. They embrace.*

SHAHRAZAD. Warm light flooded the Queen's heart when she saw her sacred children, after the darkness she had suffered for so many years.

The Story without an Ending

Dawn.

The Palace.

SHAHRAZAD. My Lord, this story shows the pain that follows, when a king acts without thinking and shuts his ears to the truth.

SHAHRAYAR. A king can lose his way like anyone else. But he can find his way back when the door to his heart is opened.

Pause.

DINARZAD. What story will you have for us tonight, Sister?

Enter the VIZIER.

VIZIER. The Headsman awaits your command, My Lord.

SHAHRAZAD. Tonight I had planned to tell a special story about another King who loses his way. It is called 'The Story

without an Ending'. But, although it is very short, I can't
seem to remember it. The well of my stories has run dry. I fear
I must go to the Headsman.

SHAHRAYAR. The Headsman cannot act without Royal decree.

SHAHRAZAD. But haven't you sworn that if the well of my
stories runs dry, I must be killed?

Silence.

Vizier, didn't you hear the King say this?

VIZIER. Well…

SHAHRAZAD. Didn't you?

VIZIER. I did.

SHAHRAZAD. Sister, you heard this, didn't you?

DINARZAD. Yes.

SHAHRAZAD. Unless the King is not a man of his word, I must
go to the Headsman.

SHAHRAYAR. Curses on your impudence. Go then, imbecile.
GET OUT! Vizier, see it done!

VIZIER. Yes, My Lord.

They exit. SHAHRAYAR *is alone. As he searches for things
to do, he becomes lonely and scared. Characters from the
stories visit the room. They move around him, speaking frag-
ments of lines from their stories. He tries to block them out.*

The BEGGAR *stumbles past.*

VIZIER (*from 'The Story of the Envious Sisters'*). Laws are
made to punish crimes.

Two of the DOGS *from 'The Wife Who Wouldn't Eat' run past
with some of the forty* THIEVES.

Some SNAKES *from 'Es-Sindibad the Sailor' appear.*

BIRD. I know who you really are. And I can tell you. It's not
who you think you are.

MARJANAH *dances by.*

ES-SINDIBAD. Till that moment I believed I would never leave the valley alive, but now I started to see a way out.

An eagle from 'Es-Sindibad the Sailor' swirls around him.

ALI BABA. OPEN SESAME!

The room is now full of characters from SHAHRAZAD's stories.

SHAHRAYAR. Shahrazad! Shahrazad! Come back here! Vizier, Headsman, stop! Stop! STOP!

The characters exit.

SHAHRAZAD, DINARZAD, VIZIER *and the rest of the Royal Court enter.*

SHAHRAZAD. You called, Your Majesty?

SHAHRAYAR. Wife, if you insist on following this ridiculous course, I shall not stand in your way.

SHAHRAZAD. Thank you, Your Majesty.

SHAHRAYAR. I am a man of my word.

SHAHRAZAD. And a king's word is as precious as water.

SHAHRAYAR. But before you go, I have one last request.

SHAHRAZAD. Certainly. How may I be of help?

SHAHRAYAR. Try to remember your story. 'The Story without an Ending'.

SHAHRAZAD. I'll see what I can do. (*She thinks hard.*) Very well, now.

Listen...

Once there was a strong, brave King who loved to laugh. One day, he was betrayed by his foolish wife and lost all his love of women and his happiness. A lonely black night fell in his heart and his soul was possessed by a dark demon. 'There is not a single good woman anywhere on the face of the earth!' he would cry.

Although he looked the same on the outside, on the inside, the good King of old was replaced by a cruel, merciless tyrant.

Every night he would marry a different woman, and the next morning he would have her killed. This way, no one could ever cheat on him again and he was safe. Darkness spread from his heart around the Palace and hung heavy over the city. Many young women died. The people feared for their daughters and grew angry and confused. 'Where has our big-hearted King disappeared to?' they asked.

Now, the King's Vizier had two daughters and the eldest daughter was blessed with a magic power. Fate had decreed that she use this magic power to slay the dark demon in the King's soul and bring the daylight back to his world. When she saw him she knew that she was also fated to love him, with a love as true as the stars and as mysterious as the moon. This woman was called Shahrazad and her magic was the magic of stories.

Night after moonlit night, she would pour the magic medicine of her stories into his ears. And little by little, day started to break in his heart and a tiny flower laid its precious roots there. Before long, the daughters of the city walked freely in the sunshine. And news that the King no longer lived in darkness travelled across the land like a white horse of hope and over the sparkling sea, bathing those that heard it in warm light.

After a long, long time, the Queen found that she was expecting the King's baby. When she had told him her stories for one thousand and one nights, she tested the King to see if the flower in his heart had bloomed and whether he was ready to save the life of his wife and unborn child.

SHAHRAYAR (*to* SHAHRAZAD). When the King heard this news, he realised that he loved Shahrazad more than any word could say, book could show or story could tell. So he asked her if she could find it in her heart to forgive him for all the terrible things he had done and whether she could help him to make amends.

SHAHRAZAD (*to* SHAHRAYAR). And she replied that the time for suffering was over.

SHAHRAYAR. Vizier.

VIZIER. Yes, My Lord?

SHAHRAYAR. Publish in the city that King Shahrayar has lifted the death sentence on Queen Shahrazad.

VIZIER. Certainly, My Lord.

SHAHRAYAR. And that she is expecting the King's baby.

VIZIER. Yes, My Lord.

SHAHRAYAR. Oh, and Vizier?

VIZIER. Yes, My Lord?

SHAHRAYAR. Have the day off.

VIZIER. Yes, My Lord.

SHAHRAYAR. Now, let us celebrate the freedom of our gracious Queen.

SHAHRAZAD. And the welcome return of the good King.

They kiss.

Dance. A celebration of rebirth.

After dance. Full COMPANY *join for…*

Epilogue

ACTOR 1. Celebrations spread throughout the land…

ACTOR 2. with eating and drinking and dancing for many days.

ACTOR 3. Afterwards, in honour of the young woman who had lost their lives…

ACTOR 4. the King called together his scribes and scholars…

ACTOR 5. and ordered them to write down every one of Shahrazad's enchanting stories into a book.

ACTOR 6. One story for each of the young women…

ACTOR 7. and one story for each night that the King's heart lived in darkness.

SHAHRAYAR. And the book lived longer than the King…

SHAHRAZAD. and Shahrazad...

DINARZAD. and their children...

ACTOR 8. and their children's children...

ACTOR 9. even the city itself.

ACTOR 10. And they called this book *Alf Layla wa Layla*...

ACTOR 11. *One Thousand and One Nights.*

ACTOR 12. But even now, when the desert sky is as dark as doom...

ACTOR 13. and the sand glows silver in the moonlight...

ACTOR 14. on the site where the old city used to be...

ACTOR 15. you can hear the sweet voice of a beautiful young woman, weaving magical tales into the night.

SHAHRAZAD. Listen...

Lights out.

The End.